MÁS ANTES

FLORENCIO MESTAS, SON OF NAPOLEÓN AND EUJELIA MESTAS, OF CABEZÓN, N.M., PLAYING THE BANJO FOR HIS TWO SISTERS, C. 1928. PHOTO COURTESY OF EDUMENIO LOVATO.

MÁS
ANTES

HISPANIC FOLKLORE OF THE
RÍO PUERCO VALLEY

Collected and Translated by Nasario García.

MUSEUM OF NEW MEXICO PRESS • SANTA FE

DEDICATED TO

JAN, MICHELE, AND RAQUEL

Manufactured in the United States of America.
Designed and composed by Susan Surprise
10 9 8 7 6 5 4 3 2 1

Library of Congress Cataloging-in-Publication Data
    García, Nasario.
        Mas Antes: hispanic folklore of the Río Puerco Valley/collected and
    translated by Nasario García.
            p.   cm.
        Text in English and New Mexican Spanish.
        ISBN 0-89013-320-4 (c). — ISBN 0-89013-323-9 (p)
        1. Mexican Americans — New Mexico — Río Puerco Valley (Río Arriba
    County-Socorro County) — Folklore. 2. Folk literature — New Mexico —
    Río Puerco Valley (Río Arriba County-Socorro County) 3. Río Puerco
    Valley (Río Arriba County-Socorro County, N.M.) — Social life and
    customs. I. Title.
    GR111.M49G37 1997
    398'.089'6872078991 — dc21   97-27785
                                                                          CIP

MUSEUM OF NEW MEXICO PRESS
Post Office Box 2087
Santa Fe, New Mexico 87504

TABLE OF

CONTENTS

ACKNOWLEDGMENTS

ABOVE ALL, I THANK THE PEOPLE OF THE RÍO PUERCO VALLEY, MANY of whom I knew as a child while growing up in Guadalupe, for sharing graciously and unselfishly the folklore in this collection. Many of them were as flattered as I was pleased to literally dig out ballads, wedding songs, and other pieces of folklore that had been stored in footlockers and forgotten. Others were amazed that I would ask them to recite a poem. What they shared will enlighten many of us for a long time to come. For this I am extremely grateful. I also wish to express my appreciation to Ronald E. Latimer, former Director, Museum of New Mexico Press; Mary Wachs, Editorial Director; Susan Surprise, Designer; and to Press staff for their support and guidance on this project. In addition, I extend special thanks to Jenifer Blakemore for her critical eye and editorial suggestions.

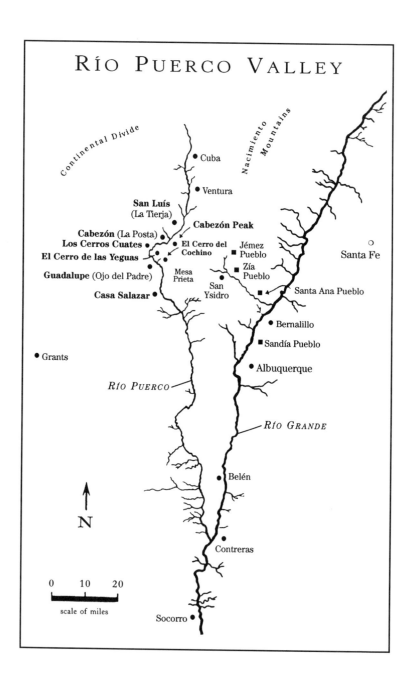

Río Puerco Valley

Continental Divide

Nacimiento Mountains

Cuba

Ventura

San Luís
(La Tierja)

Cabezón Peak

Cabezón (La Posta)
Los Cerros Cuates

El Cerro del
Cochino

Jémez
Pueblo

Santa Fe

El Cerro de las Yeguas

Zía
Pueblo

Guadalupe (Ojo del Padre)

Mesa
Prieta

San
Ysidro

Santa Ana Pueblo

Casa Salazar

Bernalillo

Sandía Pueblo

Grants

Albuquerque

Río Puerco

Río Grande

Belén

N

Contreras

0   10   20

scale of miles

Socorro

FOREWORD

*M*ÁS *ANTES*, DR. NASARIO GARCÍA'S COLLECTION OF NEW MEXICAN folklore from the Río Puerco Valley, supplements three other studies by him on the same subject: *Recuerdos de los viejitos: Tales of the Río Puerco Valley* (1987), *Abuelitos: Stories of the Río Puerco Valley* (1992), and *Tata: A Voice from the Río Puerco* (1994), all of which were published by the University of New Mexico Press in collaboration with the Historical Society of New Mexico. These works are records of various aspects of Hispanic folk life in the Río Puerco Valley in west-central New Mexico.

This area was first settled in the late 1760s during Governor Tomás Vélez Cachupín's second term in office. In *Recuerdos de los viejitos*, New Mexico archivist and historian Dr. Myra Ellen

Jenkins referred to the first settlers as "land-poor" residents from the Río Grande area of New Mexico. These people are also identified in "An Anonymous Statistical Report on New Mexico in 1765." This report, published by Dr. Donald C. Cutter of the University of New Mexico Department of History, appeared in the *New Mexico Historical Review* for October 1975. It gives the number of families and the population figures for each community, as well as for the province of New Mexico, for that year.

One settlement in the valley, San Fernando del Río Puerco, is listed as having thirty-nine families and a population of Spaniards and *gente de razón* totaling 154 persons. In Colonial New Spain, the term *gente de razón* was applied to civilized people other than Spaniards, whom one took for granted were civilized. In most cases the term included *criollos* (New Spain–born sons and daughters of Spaniards), *mestizos* (those born of Spanish and Indian parentage), and sometimes even *castas* (those born of mixed bloods other than *mestizos*).

The colonists in the Río Puerco Valley repeatedly resettled their lands. This was due to incursions by marauding Apaches from the Gila River country in the south and continuous molestations by Navajo neighbors in the north and northwest. The area then lay deserted for almost one hundred years. Then, in 1867, descendants of the original settlers started out from the central valley of the Río Grande in New Mexico and established ranches in what became Casa Salazar, Cabezón, and Guadalupe and sometime later San Luis.

It was here that the nineteenth-century colonists settled down in an Arcadian environment to start an agricultural life based on hard work and neighborly cooperation. The modicum of success the people of this later settlement enjoyed with their small farms and limited sheep and cattle pursuits lasted some seventy years and ended with the Great Depression.

In the 1930s, due to unavoidable circumstances, including droughts and new federal laws governing pasture lands and soil conservation practices, Río Puerco Hispanics had no other recourse than to give up their homes, their farms, and their grazing lands. By the 1950s, except for the few who were able to remain, most of the farmer-ranchers had sold their stock and farm implements and left.

In the last forty years, most of the former residents of the valley have passed away. A few who were living in Albuquerque and its environs in the 1970s were contacted by Dr. García. He recorded their voices together, as well as those of his parents, grandparents, and close relatives—all of whom had resided at some time in the Río Puerco area. As a young student and collector of New Mexican folklore, Dr. García was able to save from oblivion a large corpus of his people's customs and memorabilia that might have never been collected.

Throughout the pages of *Más Antes*, we are made aware of his informants' religious fervor, their complete trust in God, and their respect for the teachings of His Church. We enjoy the texts of their stories, as well as the lyrics of their favorite songs and ballads. Most of all we are charmed and enchanted with the words and idiomatic expressions they used, many of which date from fifteenth- and sixteenth-century Spain.

Más Antes is a marvelous mosaic of traditions, language, and oral history and literature that represents the rich legacy the residents of the Río Puerco Valley have left for all to enjoy.

Rubén Cobos, Professor Emeritus
The University of New Mexico

HILLTOP VIEW OF SAN JOSÉ CHURCH AND CEMETERY, CABEZÓN, N.M., 1958.
PHOTO COURTESY OF JEROLD GWAYN WIDDISON.

THE NASARIO P. AND AGAPITA L. GARCÍA HOUSE
(LEFT), BUILT IN 1935. THE TEODORO AND EMILIA P.
GARCÍA HOUSE (RIGHT), C. 1924, GUADALUPE, N.M.
EL CERRO DEL CHIVATO IN BACKGROUND.
PHOTO BY THE AUTHOR.

NASARIO P. GARCÍA'S NEW 1948
CHEVROLET. GUADALUPE, N.M., 1948.
PHOTO BY THE AUTHOR.

INTRODUCTION

As I look back at my childhood in Guadalupe in the Río Puerco Valley when my community and the other three villages, Cabezón, Casa Salazar, and San Luis, were bustling with activity, myriad remembrances pop into my mind. While I recall the pleasant aspects of these memories, I remember that life was not always charitable to us in our daily lives. Poverty, tragedies, severe winters, and summer droughts challenged the people as they struggled to eke out an existence as farmers and ranchers. To ignore this harsh reality is folly; it merely propagates a romanticized view of our state. As Don Quixote showed us, life is a double-edged sword.

Recollections, like facts, can reflect a vivid past, provided one is honest as he embarks upon that retrospective venture. The foremost goal in assembling *Más Antes: Hispanic Folklore of the Río Puerco Valley*, was to bring to the fore a repertoire of folklore that was *más antes*, or once upon a time, very much a part of each inhabitants *raison d'être*. A slice of social, cultural, linguistic, and religious past is manifest in the people's own oral and written words, but their survival is challenged daily.

Folklore serves as a kind of cultural framework within which we fit the various entities commonly called *historias* or *cuentos* (stories), *dichos* (folk sayings), *adivinanzas* (riddles), *corridos* (ballads), and other facets of Hispanic folklore that have existed in Northern New Mexico since the sixteenth century. These venues are mirrors that reflect the colorful local traditions, customs, manners, and speech that are characteristic of the Río Puerco Valley. Folklore was popular among the young and old long before the ultimate demise of the second settlement in the late 1950s.

The first settlement began in the 1760s at a time when the Río Puerco Valley was dominated by Navajos. It was then that Governor Tomás Vélez Cachupín approved several farming and grazing grants for people from the Río Grande Valley who had petitioned him for the land. The grants were on the periphery of Navajo lands, and Hispanic settlers endured periodic Indian attacks on their farms and homes. The forces of nature were no less relentless. Farming was done without irrigation and farmers were completely dependent upon Mother Nature for rain. Growing squash, corn, pinto beans, and crops was challenging; raising cattle and sheep was less trying because pasturage was plentiful.

The settlement continued with moderate success, if not tenuously, for some one hundred years. Relations between Indians and Hispanics were at best bellicose. After all, Hispanics were intruders bent on wresting someone else's land to claim as their own. The Homestead Act of 1862, enacted by Congress of the United States, made available to settlers public lands in the West. This included land in the territory of New Mexico. Typically, land was parceled out in 160-acre lots. This government action further exacerbated the weak relationships between Hispanics and Indians. Tranquility in Hispanic settlements did not materialize until the federal government established in 1868 the Navajo Reservation. A peaceful coexistence between Hispanics and Indians allowed settlers to return in the 1860s and 1870s to Casa Salazar, Cabezón, Guadalupe, and San Luis.

It was in the early 1880s that my paternal grandfather migrated with his parents and the rest of his family from Algodones, north of Albuquerque, to Casa Salazar in the Río Puerco Valley. Census records show that by 1880 Casa Salazar was well established with some two hundred inhabitants. Guadalupe had a population of 161 people, and San Luis claimed only ninety-six inhabitants. As Cabezón's population was not enumerated separately, its true count is unclear.

In 1910, Guadalupe and Casa Salazar's combined populations numbered 357 people, only four fewer than in 1880, so the number of inhabitants in the two villages remained constant during this thirty-year period. The populations of San Luis, which was also called La Tijera, and Cabezón, a settlement sometimes referred to as La Posta, were not enumerated separately. Their combined population figures were added to La Ventana's, south of Cuba. One can only conjecture that these towns' populations remained unchanged between 1880 and 1910.

The population began to dwindle after World War I when young servicemen, having completed their tours of duty, refused to return to farm life. The scarcity of water coupled with meager crops added to the exodus of people. This phenomenon gained impetus with the drastic droughts of the 1930s, by land grazing restrictions legislated by the Taylor Grazing Act of 1934, and by the destruction in 1939 of the makeshift dam, only to be exacerbated with the advent of the World War II and the Korean War shortly thereafter. Few young men were willing to return to the valley to eke out an existence on the farm. They had experienced city life far from their rural home, and their preference for urban living was firm and unequivocal. Prior to these last two wars, some families had already abandoned the Río Puerco Valley because earning a living as farmers and ranchers was no longer possible. Although they yearned for a better life, what awaited them beyond their valley provoked uncertainty and apprehension.

Most of the men were unskilled laborers without formal education, and they found modest jobs that paid no more than minimum wage. Some went to work for the Santa Fe Railroad shops in Albuquerque; there the pay was decent. Others worked for Southern Union Gas Company, Crane O'Fallon Company, the city of Albuquerque, and the State Highway Department. Most heads of households earned a respectable living (few wives worked) and bought houses for their families as they struggled to raise a family in a setting alien to and apart from the rural environment they had once called home.

As the crow flies, the Río Puerco Valley is about forty miles northwest of Albuquerque. Today one must travel on State Highway 44, northwest of Bernalillo, toward Cuba before turning onto State Highway 279 to reach the first of what were once four thriving villages: San Luis, Cabezón, Guadalupe, and Casa Salazar. In their heyday each village had its own church (those of San Luis and Cabezón remain standing) complemented by a *placita*, or village, where the splendor of many fiestas unfolded. The area with which we are concerned stretches from Casa Salazar in the south to San Luis in the north, and it measures approximately twenty miles.

As one enters the valley, the plains and mesas around San Luis are what one sees first, and the Río Puerco gradually carves its course in the dry, desolate, and austere landscape toward Cabezón, which lies hidden behind neighboring hills. Cabezón Peak, a dormant volcano with an altitude of some 8,000 feet, lies menacingly in the background.

Between Cabezón, Guadalupe, and Casa Salazar, the landscape is peppered with volcanic plugs such as Los Cerros Cuates (The Twin Peaks), El Cerro de las Yeguas (The Mares' Peak), and El Cerro del Cochino (Hog's Peak) that lie in the distance like smaller but friendly giants mimicking Cabezón Peak. Surrounding these dark blue plugs are mesas, ravines, *arroyos* (creeks), hills, and buttes with an array of vegetation. The most common types of vegetation in the Río Puerco Valley are piñon (a species of pine), juniper, shortgrass, and sagebrush. Broom snakeweed, with its yellow bloom, covers the ground in the spring. Several varieties of cacti dot the terrain.

Rain was the principal commodity in the Río Puerco Valley; it was talked about and prayed for almost on a daily basis. One's success or failure hinged on rain as it was critical for the survival of crops and livestock upon which the people were dependent. The relationship between man, land, and nature was oftentimes not favorable toward man, but the people of the Río Puerco Valley were resilient. With their faith in God and their devotion to their families, they managed to have fun and be philosophical about life. This is what comes to us in the folklore contained in the following chapters.

Today, approximately two-thirds of the contributors to *Más Antes: Hispanic Folklore of the Río Puerco Valley* are deceased. Those who are alive are quite old and only a few are in good health, but they look back on their lives in the valley with contentment and satisfaction, as did those who passed away. Rarely does one hear complaints about the lives they led. In their hearts they believe that God is responsible for their destiny. They are mindful that *"El hombre propone y Dios dispone"* (Man proposes and God disposes), and it is this philosophical outlook, concomitant with their profound religious convictions, that sustained them during both good and hard times. Today, Cabezón, Casa Salazar, Guadalupe, and San Luis are ghost towns and, as such, symbols of a period of history that is sealed in the minds of former occupants.

The folklore in this book epitomizes a variety of sentiments enjoyed, suffered, and endured by the Río Puercoans. This array of emotions can be witnessed, felt, and appreciated in the following historias, dichos, corridos, *entriegas* (wedding songs), and the like. Much can be learned from the folklore old-timers shared with us as it tells of their language, their customs, and their traditions that they inherited from their parents and grandparents. Each component, be it a folk saying or a ballad, is a jewel, as it were, in the treasure trove of Hispanic culture in Northern New Mexico.

In 1965, after spending the academic year of 1964–65 taking doctoral courses at the University of Granada in Andalucía, Spain, I returned home to Albuquerque, where I ventured into a bookstore. There I found a copy of Jack D. Rittenhouse's just-published book, *Cabezón: A New Mexico Ghost Town* (Santa Fe: Stagecoach Press, 1965). Seeing a book about the region where I had grown up and then reading about the people whom I knew as a young boy, intrigued me. Indeed, my curiosity was piqued when I noticed the similarity in the folklore of Andalucía, Spain, and that of the Río Puerco Valley in New Mexico. Parading the Virgin of Guadalupe, our patron saint, around the village or up and down the valley during the summer months or taking Nuestro Señor de Esquipulas, my paternal grandmother's favorite *santo* (carved wood sculpture), into the cornfields to plead for rain was no different than what I had witnessed in southern Spain. The humble and religious people I saw in Andalucía were just like those from the Río Puerco Valley. My role as a spectator in Andalucía obviated for me the close relationship between two geographically separate yet sister worlds. This experience induced me to re-explore the valley where I had spent the formative years of my life.

In 1968, a neophyte in oral literature, I borrowed a reel-to-reel tape recorder and proceeded to interview my paternal grandparents. I undertook no more oral interviews until 1977. Since that time I have interviewed dozens of former Río Puerco Valley residents in order to tell their story. Some of these materials appeared in my books, *Recuerdos de los viejitos*, *Abuelitos*, and *Tata*.

Más Antes: Hispanic Folklore of the Río Puerco Valley provides additional material to add to the folklore annals of New Mexico. It features informants who did not appear in my previous works, and it brings together for the first time a variety of folklore never before credited to Río Puerco residents. Some of the materials, such as the wills and the eulogy, rarely appear in folklore publications; hence, they are not commonly known to the general reader in New Mexico or elsewhere. Each interview was conducted in Spanish, the people's native language; reminiscing frequently was prefaced with this phrase: *más antes*, which means "a long time ago." The English translations reflect the meaning and spirit of what the interviewees conveyed. In pieces such as ballads or wedding songs, the translations' most important aspect is communicating what is stated in Spanish and not reproducing the rhyme scheme per se.

To realize that each featured form was felt and experienced by all of the informants at one time or another is to fully appreciate the value of folklore in its linguistic, social, cultural, and religious contexts. Herein lies the legacy of those who lived in the Río Puerco Valley.

NASARIO P. GARCÍA
AND HIS OLDER
SISTERS, GUADALUPE,
N.M. FROM LEFT,
TEODORITA,
JULIANITA, AND
PETRITA, C. 1920–21.
PHOTO: AUTHOR'S
PRIVATE COLLECTION.

AGAPITA L. AND
NASARIO P. GARCÍA,
1948,
PHOTOGRAPHED
SOUTH OF CABEZÓN
PEAK NEAR LAGUNA
DE DON RICARDO.
PHOTO BY
THE AUTHOR.

DAY OF *MATANZA*, GUADALUPE, C. 1922–24. FROM LEFT, TEODORITA GARCÍA,
NASARIO P. GARCÍA, LEOPOLDO GARCÍA (NO RELATION), EMILIA P. GARCÍA (MOTHER),
FILOMENA GALLEGOS, A FRIEND, TEODORO GARCÍA (FATHER), AND PETRITA GARCÍA.
PHOTO COURTESY OF TEODORITA GARCÍA-RUELAS.

CHAPTER 1

DICHOS

FOLK SAYINGS

Iɴ *Doɴ Quɪxote*, Mɪɢuᴇʟ ᴅᴇ Cᴇʀᴠᴀɴᴛᴇs's ᴄʟᴀssɪᴄ ɴᴏᴠᴇʟ, Doɴ Quixote once said to his squire Sancho Panza, "Sancho, it seems to me that no proverb exists that is not beholden to truth, because all proverbs are axiomatic expressions taken from the mother of all sciences, which is experience in and of itself." In the Old Testament Proverbs 1:6, King Solomon underscores the element of truth in proverbs: "To understand a proverb, and the interpretation; the words of the wise, and their dark sayings."

Great thinkers and writers have always availed themselves of these expressions to communicate certain thoughts. Many of the ancients' proverbs have come down to us sometimes in different forms but with their initial meaning intact. In Proverbs 16:2, we read, "All the ways of a man are clean in his own eyes; but the LORD weigheth the spirits." This may be interpreted as *"El hombre propone y Dios dispone"* (Man proposes and God disposes).

In interviews I have conducted with old men and women from the Río Puerco Valley and other rural areas of New Mexico, someone invariably alluded to a dicho in the Scriptures and once in a while referred to *"el Gordo"* or *"el Panzudo,"* that is, Sancho Panza, known for his penchant for dichos. A cursory look at Spanish literature from the Middle Ages to the Golden Age (ca. 1140–1680) reveals that dichos have played an important role in several classical works. In *El libro de buen amor* by Juan Ruiz (1283?–1351?), dichos such as *"Lo poco y bien dicho penetra el corazón"* (Little and well said penetrates the heart, or A word to the wise is sufficient) abound. In Fernando de Roja's Renaissance classic, *La Celestina* (1492), dichos are frequently used by the principal character, Celestina, in her dealings with both her under-lings and with members of the upper class. The anonymous author of Spain's first important picaresque novel, *Lazarillo de Tormes* (1554), also employed dichos. In the very first episode, a young boy named Lazarillo is admonished by one of several masters, a blind man, who comments on man's inhumanity to man when he says, *"Necio, aprende: que el mozo del ciego un punto ha de saber más que el diablo,"* or "Pay attention, you dolt, for the blind man's guide must be one step ahead of the devil himself." And last but not least I mention again *Don Quixote* (1605/15) because, like *Lazarillo de Tormes*, it coincides with the colonial period in New Mexico, and one finds evidence of these books' linguistic influence in our state. Aurelio M. Espinosa suggests in *The Folklore of Spain in the American Southwest* (Norman: University of Oklahoma Press, 1985) that dichos such as *"Cada oveja con su pareja"* (Birds of a feather flock together) and *"De lo dicho al hecho hay gran trecho"* (It is easier said than done) found in Spanish America and New Mexico can be traced back to *Don Quixote*. Many other dichos indigenous to Spain can be found in Hispanic countries of the New World where they have enjoyed a long-standing tradition among Spanish speakers. Indeed, one can hear dichos among the old-timers of New Mexico today.

While many dichos such as those found in *Don Quixote* share a universal commonality and exhibit minimal distortion in contextual meaning or syntactical structure, some issue directly from specific regions and local communities. Their appeal is sometimes limited to a defined area and its distinct population. A multitude of dichos, for example, was born right here in New Mexico's Río Puerco Valley.

After more than four hundred years since the Spaniards' arrival in New Mexico, the dicho is alive and well. They are still heard on a daily basis among denizens of rural villages in Northern New Mexico and among former residents of the Río Puerco Valley.

The word *dicho* has its roots in the Spanish verb *decir*, which means "to say," and it is derived from the Latin *dicere*. *Dicho*, which is the past participle of *decir*, is what is commonly known as the pluperfect construction formed with the verb "to have." Hence "I have said" translates into *"Yo he dicho."* The word dicho in folkloric terminology, particularly as it relates to New Mexico, means a folk saying. At times, albeit on rare occasions, the words *refrán*, *proverbio*, and *adagio* are used in lieu of dicho. However, the latter is by far the most popular among common people. Time and again I heard as a child in the Río Puerco Valley older men and women say, *"Había un dicho que decía,"* "There was a saying that went like this."

Some dichos were passed on from one generation to another, so many are quite old. Others are relatively new. Nevertheless, dichos reflect a certain individuality that emanates from a way of life, a way of thinking, and a philosophy specific to the people who utter them. The use of dichos is personal and colloquial, and it is inextricably bound to one's language. For these and other reasons, the dichos a particular population uses convey much more than what one may perceive as a reader. That is because folk sayings function on two levels: the literal and the figurative or abstract. Hence, a dicho may convey or imply more than one thing, depending on the context within which it is offered. How a user frames a dicho may occur almost instinctively, without any preconceived notion. All in all, dichos are sophisticated forms by which a people's truth and wisdom are expressed.

By examining folk sayings popular among former residents of this New Mexico valley, we gain a sense of the world these people inhabited, a world imbued with pragmatism and sound philosophical judgment. Men and women believed in these sayings and lived by them as though they were articles of faith. Some rhyme and are unique and some can be traced back to Spain or Mexico, but most of the dichos in this collection are native to the villages of the Río Puerco Valley.

Each dicho is presented first in Spanish, and it is accompanied by a literal translation of the folk saying and then by an expression in English that best resembles the saying's inherent meaning. A number of these fascinating expressions are self-explanatory; others require contemplation and analysis. The dichos included in this chapter address such issues as education, respect, religion, connivance, and embarrassment, but each one pertains in some way to human behavior.

Dichos are charged expressions that were never explained. Somehow we divined what they meant, we acknowledged their power, and we grasped their philosophical thrust. Invariably, dichos were put into practice particularly when parents found themselves in a situation in which they had to advise their children. They were often used to convey, with concision and subtlety, a specific message. Even today when I visit my father I listen to him intently because of the way he proffers profound wisdom, much of it conveyed by a smattering of dichos. Such sayings are indeed part of his persona, and as long as Spanish is spoken in New Mexico, dichos shall thrive among those who approach life in a philosophical and pragmatic way.

DICHOS — FOLK SAYINGS[1]

ADRIÁN CHÁVEZ

Confianza ni a mi agüelo. ([I have] confidence not even in my grandfather.) **Trust no one.**

El mero vender era no comprar. (Merely selling meant not buying.) **Self-sufficiency was the name of the game.**

Suerte te de Dios, que saber poco importa. (May God bring you luck, for a little knowledge is dangerous.) **God's blessing is better than knowledge.**

NASARIO GARCÍA

De las dos no se hace una. (You can't make one thing from two.) **You can't make heads or tails out of it.**

De noche todos los gatos son pardos. (At night, all cats are gray.) **At night, everything looks the same.**

De tal palo, tal estilla. (From such a stick, such a splinter.) **Like father, like son.**

Del dicho al hecho hay gran trecho. (From word to deed is a great distance.) **It's easier said than done.**

El gato que duerme no caza ratones. (The cat that sleeps does not catch mice.) **The early bird gets the worm.**

El que más tiene más quiere. (He who has more, wants more.) **The more you have, the more you want.**

El que no llora no mama. (The baby who does not cry does not get to nurse.) **The squeaky wheel gets the grease.**

El que sale a bailar pierde su lugar. (He who gets up to dance loses his seat.) **You can't be in two places at once.**

Él ya no suena ni truena. (He no longer cracks or makes thunder.) **He can't cut the mustard anymore.**

En boca cerrada no entra mosca. (A closed mouth lets no flies in.) **Silence is golden.**

Estar cortao de la misma tela. (To be cut from the same cloth.) **They are cut from the same cloth.**

Estar cortao por la misma tijera. (To be cut with the same scissors.) **They are one of a kind.**

Haz las cosas al revés y las haces otra vez. (Do things backwards and you'll do them again.) **Haste makes waste. Measure twice, cut once.**

No hay mal que por bien no venga. (There is no ill that doesn't bring something good.) **Every cloud has a silver lining.**

Panza llena corazón contento. (A full belly, a happy heart.) **The way to a man's heart is through his stomach.**

Perro que ladra no muerde. (A dog that barks does not bite.) **His bark is worse than his bite.**

ADELITA GONZALES

Cuando Dios no quiere, santos no pueden. (When God is unwilling, the saints can't do anything.) **If God is unwilling, even the saints can't perform miracles.**

AGAPITA LÓPEZ-GARCÍA

Dime con quién andas y te diré quién eres. (Tell me who you run around with and I'll tell you who you are.) **A person is known by the company he keeps.**

La flor arriba y la jedentina abajo. (The flower above and the stench below.) **Appearances aren't always what they seem to be.**

Lo que ustedes hagan con sus padres, sus hijos harán con ustedes. (Whatever you do to your parents, your children will do to you.) **Monkey see, monkey do.**

Naide se va d'este mundo sin pagar las que debe. (No one leaves this earth without paying what he owes.) **No one departs this earth without paying his debts.**

No escupas al cielo que en la cara te caidrá. (Don't spit at the sky because it [the saliva] will land on your face.) **Don't try to harm someone for you may fail and also inflict harm upon yourself.**

No todas las uñas de los dedos son iguales. (Not all the fingernails of the fingers are equal.) **Your children are not all the same.**

EDUMENIO LOVATO

A donde fueres has lo que vieres. (Wherever you go, do as you see.) **When in Rome, do as the Romans do.**

De mañana en mañana pierde la oveja la lana. (From morning to morning the sheep loses its wool.) **Don't put off until tomorrow what you can do today.**

Dios le da a cada quien la carga que El sabe cada quien la puede soportar. (God gives everyone the load that He knows they can carry.) **God won't give you a burden greater than you can bear.**

Donde tienes tu tesoro, allí tienes tu corazón. (Wherever your treasure lies, there is your heart.) **Your heart lies in that which you treasure.**

Febrero loco, marzo airiento, abril llovioso, sacan a mayo florido y hermoso. (Crazy February, windy March, and rainy April bring out a flower-filled and beautiful May.) **April showers bring May flowers.**

Muchos pocos hacen un mucho. (Many littles make a lot.) **Many hands make light work. The whole is greater than the parts.**

No dejes camino por vereda, ni vereda por de reserva. (Don't abandon the road for a trail nor a trail for something unknown.) **A bird in the hand is worth two in the bush.**

No hay mal que bien no traiga. (There is no ill that does not bring something good.) **There is hope even in something negative. Something good comes of even bad situations.**

Para desperados males, desperados remedios. (For desperate ills, desperate remedies.) **There is a cure for everything. The cure is worse than the illness.**

Poco a poco se anda lejos. (Little by little one walks a long way.) **One step at a time gets you a long way.**

Poco a poco se are el terreno. (Little by little the land is sown.) **Little by little, all the seeds are sown.**

Por la calle de mañana se edifica la ciudad de nunca. (Going down tomorrow's road means building the city of "never.") **Don't put off until tomorrow what you can do today.**

Tanto baja el cántaro al agua hasta que se ahoga. (The jug goes down the well so often that it finally drowns.) **One can go to the well once too often. Don't press your luck.**

Uno ha de pensar para hacer, y no hacer para pensar. (One must think before doing something and not do something to think about later.) **Think before you act instead of acting before you think.**

Uno ha de ser cuando es, porque cuando uno no es, para qué es. (One must be who one is because when one is not, what's the point?) **Don't try to be what you are not.**

SALOMÓN LOVATO

Caballo manso con caballada estraña se enseña a huir. (A tame horse learns how to run away with a strange herd of horses.) **A man is known by the company he keeps.**

El que anda con lobos a'ullar se enseña. (He who mingles with wolves learns how to howl.) **A person is judged by the company he keeps.**

No había rey ni roque ni campana que nos tocara. (There was neither king nor rook nor bell that could ring us.) **There was no one equal to us.**

No jalló leña, jalló barañas. (He didn't find wood, he found briars.) **He thought the grass was greener on the other side.**

Onde va el buey que are. (Wherever the ox goes, it is made to plow.) **The poor man has to work everywhere he goes.**

Primero rezarete, y loo bailarete. (First you must pray, and then you may dance up a storm.) **Business before pleasure.**

Vale más morir una a palos que no quedar garrotiao. (It is better to die from a good beating than to be left beaten up.) **Better to be a dead hero than a live coward.**

BENJAMÍN ("BENNY") LUCERO

Dios no castiga con palos ni azotes. (God doesn't punish with blows or beatings.) **Punishment is lame but it comes.**

NASARIO P. GARCÍA

Culebra que chilla, no pica. (A hissing snake doesn't bite.) **His bark is worse than his bite.**

Hacer lumbre pa que otro se caliente las manos. (Build a fire now so another may warm his hands.) **He's a Johnny-come-lately.**

Ir con el sombrero en la mano. (Go with your hat in your hand.) **Be polite and humble.**

Ir con la cola entre las piernas. (Go with your tail between your legs.) **He's got his tail between his legs.**

Mientras más escarba uno la mierda, más jiede. (The more you stir shit, the more it smells.) **Look for trouble and you'll find it.**

Mientras más viejo, más pendejo. (The older you get, the more stupid you are.) **Age doesn't always teach us wisdom.**

No digas nada que tú tamién tienes hijos. (Don't say anything for you also have children.) **Don't say something that will come back to haunt you.**

No hay escusao que no huele. (There is not an outhouse that doesn't smell.) **No one is perfect.**

No hay que criar uno cuervos pa que le saquen los ojos. (One must not raise crows so they can pluck out your eyes.) **Don't expect angels if you raise devils.**

Otra vez la burra al trigo. (There goes the female donkey back to the wheat.) **Here we go again.**

Ráscate y sacarás liendres. (Scratch and you shall find nits.) **Look for trouble and you'll find it.**

Se hace el sordo cuando le conviene. (He pretends he is deaf when it behooves him.) **He turns a deaf ear when it's convenient.**

Se tapa el sol con la mano. (He shades himself from the sun with his hand.) **He pretends to know nothing.**

Son días de uno y vísperas de otro. (They are days for some and evenings for others.) **Life has its pluses and minuses.**

Tanto le pica uno al burro hasta que respinga. (Poke a donkey enough times until it finally kicks.) **There is a limit to a person's patience.**

Tirar la piedra y esconder la mano. (Throw a stone and hide your hand.) **Don't pull the wool over people's eyes.**

Uno propone y Dios dispone. (One proposes and God disposes.) **God always has the last word.**

ANTOÑITA VALDEZ DE LEYBA

Pobre fiel o pobremete, pero muy contenta la gente. (No matter how poor people were, they were happy.) **They were poor but happy.**

Una mujer en su cintura a la cara se conoce que es güena. (One can tell a good woman from the waist to the face.) **A woman's character is measured from the waist up.**[2]

NOTES

1. Translations of some of the dichos come from Rubén Cobos's book *Refranes: Southwestern Spanish Proverbs* (Santa Fe: Museum of New Mexico Press, 1985).

2. If a woman wore too much makeup, she was considered by the ladies in the community to be a social spectacle.

THE EDUARDO VALDEZ FAMILY, FORMERLY FROM GUADALUPE, PICKING PIÑÓN, 1953. PHOTO COURTESY OF ADELINA VALDEZ-BACA.

METATE, C. 1850S, ONCE OWNED BY NASARIO GARCÍA'S PATERNAL GRANDMOTHER, EMILIA PADILLA GARCÍA. PHOTO BY THE AUTHOR.

CHAPTER 2

ADIVINANZAS

RIDDLES

In 1996 WHILE IN TRUJILLO, SPAIN, A COMMUNITY OF APPROXIMATELY nine thousand inhabitants in west-central Spain, I delivered at El Museo de la Coria a lecture on "Hispanic Folklore of New Mexico: A Spanish Connection." In sharing scores of folkloric elements, among them dichos and adivinanzas, I was pleasantly surprised by the audience's enthusiastic response. A number of people in attendance shared with me dichos and adivinanzas popular in their province, Extremadura. Others were intrigued and fascinated by the fact that some of the riddles in my presentation were popular in Trujillo itself. They were elated to know that their folklore had traveled across the Atlantic Ocean all the way to Northern New Mexico.

Regarding the link between New Mexico and Spain, several observations merit attention. Some of the adivinanzas in this chapter are identical to those heard in Spain and are found in collections such as *Adivinancero antológico español* (Spain: Ediciones Del Prado, 1994) by José Luis Gárfer and Concha Fernández. The following is an example of a riddle found in New Mexico and in Spain.

En alto vive,
en alto mora,
en alto teje
la tejedora.
    ¿Qué es?

She lives up-high,
she dwells up-high,
she weaves up-high,
the so-called weaver.
    What is it?

ANSWER: *La araña*/A spider

Other Spanish riddles, such as the two that follow, have changed very little in New Mexico:

En el llano está Mariano;
tiene cruz y no es cristiano.
    ¿Qué es?

Mariano is on the plains;
he has a cross but is not a Christian.
    What is it?

ANSWER: *La entraña*/A cactus

Oro parece,
plata no es,
quien no lo acierte,
bien tonto es.
¿Qué es?

It looks like gold,
it is not silver,
he who can't ascertain this,
is really dumb.
What is it?

ANSWER: *El plátano*/A banana

Still others seem to have been modified only slightly in New Mexico, but the inherent spirit within them remains unaffected. The following riddles underscore this phenomenon:

Dime quién será
que va por el mar
fumándose un puro
sin saber nadar.
¿Qué es?

Tell me who can it be
that goes by sea
smoking a cigar
without knowing how to swim.
What is it?

ANSWER: *Un barco de vapor*
A steamship

En el campo me crié,
atada con verdes lazos,
y aquel que llora por mí,
me está partiendo en pedazos.
¿Qué es?

I grew up in the countryside,
bundled together with green ribbons,
and he who cries for me,
is cutting me into pieces.
    What is it?

ANSWER: *La cebolla*/An onion

The riddle nexus between New Mexico and Spain is indisputable. However, a certain ingenuity in the composition of these folkloric jewels is at work in the New Mexican riddles whose answers are objects found in our state. References to the chile, a grinding stone, and a branding iron demonstrate this attribute. Other such references will be seen throughout this chapter.

The word *adivinanza* comes from *adivinar*, which means "to guess, to discover intuitively, to divine." Adivinanzas have been around the Southwest since colonial times and are still heard today among old-timers in the small communities of Northern New Mexico. Many people, including former residents of the Río Puerco Valley, recall riddles with fondness and delight and expound on the joy they brought to everyone be they young or old. Riddles were turned into a kind of cat-and-mouse game between grandparents, the *agüelitos*, or the *papá grande* (grandfather) and the *mamá grande* (grandmother) and their grandchildren.

Riddles involve various objects and topics, ranging from people, animals, gastronomy, music, numbers, games, vegetables, to the cosmos. The answers to riddles are not always easily determined in either Spanish or in English. If we ask someone, "What's black and white and read all over?" the color "red" is "heard" verbally and thus the guesser is led astray. Clearly, a homophone, in this case red/read, is central to the riddle's answer. Just as the play on words is critical to the sense and fun in this English riddle, such is the case in many Spanish riddles.

Like any typical riddle, the fun lies in being able to solve it by answering the question, "What is it?" Sometimes the answer lies within the clues in the riddle's lines; other times the solution must be gleaned from the riddle's context. Solving these riddles requires that one use language imaginatively. Since much wordplay is lost in the English translation, it is difficult to guess the riddle's answer regardless of one's cerebral capabilities. Familiarity with Hispanic culture and knowing where such a riddle was told help one answer the question correctly. As you divine your answers to these adivinanzas, look for these four things: a play on words, metaphors, cultural symbols, and hompohones and homonyms. These hints helped me solve riddles when I was a child.

My aunt Teodorita García-Ruelas once told me, "In every home at night, people gathered to exchange riddles. They used to pass the time telling riddles, and the one who lost, they made him pray, they made him kneel and pray . . . the Our Father, the Hail Mary." And so it was in many homes where there was no radio or television. The grandparents were the medium, and oral literature, such as riddles, was the message.

When I was a child, my maternal grandmother, Lucinda Atencio, taught me a number of riddles that are simple and of a general nature. Other riddles are more complex and have dual meanings that range from the innocent to the sexual. The risqué riddles were not shared with children; rather, they were reserved for adults, who had their own riddle sessions in the evenings after the children were asleep. Prior to her death in 1978, my grandmother shared with me both groups of riddles alluded to here; at last, she had come to consider me old enough to listen to the more erotic ones.

The adivinanzas are in alphabetical order according to the contributors' names. English translations convey the sense of each riddle, but they do not conform to the rhyme scheme established in Spanish. For those without a firm command of the Spanish language, the play on words is explained. Each riddle is followed by a short commentary that may help the reader determine the correct answer.

LUCINDA ATENCIO

> *Oro no es,*
> *plata no es.*
> *Levanta la cortina,*
> *y sabrás lo que es.*
>   *¿Qué es?*

> It's not gold,
> nor is it silver.
> Raise the curtain,
> and you'll find it for certain.
>   What is it?

ANSWER: El plátano/A banana

(The key to the answer lies in combining *plata* and *no*. *Es* (it is) merely reinforces the answer. The curtain is a metaphor for this item's covering.)

◆ ◆ ◆

> *Blanco salí de mi casa,*
> *y en el campo enverdecí.*
> *Para entrar en mi casa,*
> *de colorado me metí.*
>   *¿Qué es?*

> I left my house in white,
> and in the country turned green.
> In order to enter my house,
> I got dressed up in red.
>   What is it?

ANSWER: El chile/Chile

(The colors green and red are characteristic of this item grown in New Mexico.)

◆ ◆ ◆

Mariano está en el llano.
Tiene cruz y no es cristiano.
  ¿Qué es?

Mariano is on the plains.
Has a cross and isn't Christian.
  What is it?

ANSWER: *La entraña/*Buckhorn
or cane cactus

(A desert plant, whose configurations may resemble a cross, is personified; hence, the reference to the plant not being a Christian.)

◆ ◆ ◆

Redondito y redondón,
con ajuero y con tapón.
  ¿Qué es?

It's round and round,
with a hole and a plug.
  What is it?

ANSWER: *Una calabaza/*A pumpkin

(This riddle refers to a farm product. When one cuts around the coarse vine where it joins the vegetable of this decumbent plant, one creates a plug for the round, ball-like item.)

◆ ◆ ◆

Una vaca pasa por el mar
pegando bramidos
sin ser animal.
  ¿Qué es?

A cow floats over the ocean
mooing wildly

without being an animal.
What is it?

ANSWER: *Las nubes*/Clouds

(Only an imagined animal can float above the sea. Towering forms that harbor storms are the source of suggestive sound effects.)

◆ ◆ ◆

Redondo como una bola,
cuatrocientos hijos tengo.
Los mantengo
con la cola.
  ¿Qué es?

Round as a ball,
I have four hundred children.
I support them
with the tail.
  What is it?

ANSWER: *La cebolla*/An onion

(The key words for solving this riddle about a vegetable are *bola* (ball) and *cola* (tail).)

◆ ◆ ◆

Blanca como la nieve,
negra como la tez.
Habla sin tener boca,
y camina sin tener pies.
  ¿Qué es?

White as snow,
black as skin.
Without a mouth it talks,
and without feet it walks.
  What is it?

ANSWER: *Una carta*/A letter

(The colors black and white provide strong clues to the answer, as do the suggestions that this item communicates and travels.)

♦ ♦ ♦

Gila que gila,
por los rincones,
tú de puntitas,
y yo de talones.
    ¿Qué es?

Here and there,
throughout the corners,
I'm on my tippy-toes,
and you're on your heels.
    What is it?

ANSWER: *Una escoba*/A broom

(Imagine a person standing on their tippy-toes, reaching into corners with something pointy.)

♦ ♦ ♦

Dale que dale,
que es muncho trabajo.
Tú boca arriba,
y yo boca abajo.
    ¿Qué es?

Up and down,
my but it's lots of work.
You're on your back,
and I'm facing down.
    What is it?

ANSWER: *Un metate*/A pumice stone

(Although infused with sexual overtones, this riddle refers to an Indian or a Hispanic woman grinding corn. The question is, with what is she grinding?)

♦ ♦ ♦

Blanco salí de mi casa,
y en el campo enverdecí.
Para entrar a mi casa,
tan blanco como salí.
  ¿Qué es?

I left my house white,
and in the countryside I turned green.
In order to enter my house,
[I am] as white as when I left.
  What is it?

ANSWER: *El trigo*/Wheat flour

(This is another agricultural staple common in the Río Puerco Valley that goes full cycle in appearance, from white to white. It is used in making tortillas or bread.)

♦ ♦ ♦

Caballito de banda a banda,
que ni come ni bebe
ni anda.
  ¿Qué es?

Little horse that rocks
from side to side,
that neither eats nor drinks
nor walks.
  What is it?

ANSWER: *Un puente*/A bridge

(Like a wooden horse that rocks from side to side [or up and down], it sits on top of water but neither drinks nor walks.)

◆ ◆ ◆

Largo y peludo
y en la punta
un ñudo
   ¿Qué es?

Long and hairy
and at the tip
a knot.
   What is it?

ANSWER: *El cabresto*/A rope

(Seemingly sexual in that it suggests a penis, the object is something used by cowboys in their work with livestock.)

◆ ◆ ◆

Fui pa la plaza,
y me vine con ella.
Llegué a mi casa,
y me puse a llorar con ella.
   ¿Qué es?

I went to the plaza,
and came home with her.
I arrived home,
and began crying with her.
   What is it?

ANSWER: *La cebolla*/An onion

(While this riddle gives the impression that *ella* is a woman with whom her husband cries upon arriving home, *ella* is in fact a vegetable.)

◆ ◆ ◆

Mételo duro,
sácalo blando,
coloradito [y] relampaguiando.
  ¿Qué es?

Put it in hard,
take it out soft,
reddish like lightning.
  What is it?

ANSWER: *La marca*/A branding iron

(This riddle with a double entendre certainly alludes to sexual intercourse, but the object in question is something ranchers and cowboys use to brand their cattle or horses.)

NASARIO GARCÍA

Ya ves,
el que no me lo adivine
bien tonto es.
  ¿Qué es?

You see,
he who doesn't guess,
is indeed quite dense.
  What is it?

ANSWER: *Las llaves*/Keys

(The answer lies in the play on the words *ya* and *ves*, which when combined form *yaves*, or *llaves*. A person uses them to open locks.)

◆ ◆ ◆

Habla sin tener boca.
Camina sin tener pies.
  ¿Qué es?

Without a mouth it talks.
Without feet it walks.
What is it?

ANSWER: *La carta*/A letter

(A truncated version of a riddle discussed earlier.)

♦ ♦ ♦

Yo aquí
y
tú allá.
¿Qué es?

I'm here
and
you're there.
What is it?

ANSWER: *Una toalla*/A towel

(On the surface, this riddle appears to involve two people, but in reality the answer lies in the word formed by combining *tú* and *allá*. We use this item to dry ourselves.)

♦ ♦ ♦

Rita, Rita,
que en el monte grita,
y en su casa calladita.
¿Qué es?

Rita, oh, Rita,
who in the countryside shouts,
but at home puts up no bouts.
What is it?

ANSWER: *El hacha*/An ax

(Rita in this case is a tool one uses when harvesting wood and not the name of a woman per se. Its sounds and echoes can be heard across the land, but when in a corner at home, it rests quietly.)

◆ ◆ ◆

En alto vive,
en alto mora,
en alto teje,
la tejedora.
  ¿Qué es?

She lives up-high,
she dwells up-high,
she weaves up-high,
The so-called weaver.
  What is it?

ANSWER: *La araña*/A spider

(The crucial words are *teje* and *tejedora,* which derive from *tejer,* to weave. The weaver is something we see in high corners.)

◆ ◆ ◆

Una vieja
con un solo diente,
junta a toda su gente.
  ¿Qué es?

An old woman
with only one tooth,
brings all her people together.
  What is it?

ANSWER: *La campana*/A bell

(Vieja (old woman) and *diente* (tooth) conjure up the image of a witchlike woman, but together they are a metaphor for that which tolls, summoning all to church.)

♦ ♦ ♦

Redondito,
redondón.
No tiene tapa,
ni tapón.
¿Qué es?

It's round,
a little bit round.
It doesn't have a lid,
nor a cork.
What is it?

ANSWER: *Un anillo*/A ring

(It is small, perfectly round, and we wear it on a finger.)

♦ ♦ ♦

Mi madre tenía una sábana,
y no la podía doblar.
Mi padre tenía muncho dinero,
y no lo podía contar.
¿Qué es?

My mother had a bedsheet,
but she couldn't fold it.
My father had lots of money,
but he couldn't count it.
What is it?

ANSWER: *El cielo y las estrellas*
The sky and stars

(For the answer, consider what you see when you look at the night's canopy of darkness.)

SUSANITA RAMÍREZ DE ARMIJO

> *¿Qué Cristo en su niñez*
> *sembró una mata en el suelo?*
> *¿Quién tendrá mejor asiento*
> *que Jesucristo en el cielo?*
> *¿Qué es?*

> What plant did Christ sow
> in the ground during his childhood?
> Who has a better seat in Heaven
> than Jesus Christ?
> What is it?

ANSWER: *La corona/*
The crown of thorns

(The development of a seed into a plant is a metaphor for Christ's maturation from youth to adult. What Christ sowed was his teachings, and what was placed upon his head at the Crucifixion as a consequence of this activity has the best seat in the house.)

DAMIANO ROMERO

> *Lana sube,*
> *lana baja.*
> *¿Qué es?*

> Wool goes up,
> wool comes down.
> What is it?

ANSWER: *La navaja/*A knife

(By combining the words *lana* and *baja*, one gets *lanabaja*, which is how the answer to the puzzle is frequently pronounced.)

♦ ♦ ♦

Dos paderes blancas
y el medio es amarillo.
  ¿Qué es?

Two white walls
and the middle is yellow.
  What is it?

ANSWER: *Un huevo*/An egg

(This popular riddle describes something that is white on the outside and yellow on the inside. It was eaten on the ranch almost every day.)

EDUARDO VALDEZ

Para matar un cochino,
¿qué opina usted?
¿Qué cosa es la más necesaria?
  ¿Qué es?

To slaughter a hog,
what do you think?
What's the most necessary thing?
  What is it?

ANSWER: *Un marrano*/A hog

(Hogs were important to the self-sufficient families of the Río Puerco Valley. In this case, the pig may have the last laugh.)

NASARIO P. GARCÍA
POINTING TO THE SITE,
WEST OF CABEZÓN, WHERE
JUAN VALDEZ'S BODY WAS
DUMPED AFTER BEING
MURDERED IN 1908.
PHOTO BY THE AUTHOR.

AVELINO VALDEZ, C. 1927, MENTALLY RETARDED
SON OF JUAN VALDEZ, WAS LEFT AN ORPHAN TO
ROAM THE RÍO PUERCO VALLEY. PHOTO COURTESY
OF EDUMENIO LOVATO.

CHAPTER 3

CUENTOS

STORIES

I_N_ DISCUSSING STORIES POPULAR IN THE RÍO PUERCO VALLEY, ONE IS inclined to relate them to legends such as *"La Llorona,"* "The Wailing Woman," or to those stories whose roots can be traced to Spain, Mexico, Persia, or India, but that is hardly the case in the oral prose collected from former residents. Most of their stories have their roots in the region, and they emanate from personal experiences often imbued with folkloric overtures.

The heinous death of Juan Valdez in Cabezón in 1908 as recounted here by Benny Lucero in "They Murdered Him with an Ax" is a classic example of this folkloric phenomenon. Other stories about Juan Valdez have appeared in my *Recuerdos de los viejitos: Tales of the Río Puerco*, and all of them contain gruesome details of a tragic death that stunned Cabezón and the entire Río Puerco Valley. Indeed, a man's destiny is every bit as unpredictable as it is tragic or sad. "Avelino," also by Benny Lucero, is the story of Juan Valdez's mentally retarded son who, after being left an orphan, was destined to roam from home to home between Cabezón and San Luis performing menial jobs in exchange for food.

The stories, *historias*, as the Río Puercoan called them, are told in a simple and straightforward style, and the language at times does contain archaisms or expressions indigenous to New Mexico or the Río Puerco Valley in particular.

CUENTOS

BENJAMÍN ("BENNY") LUCERO

Avelino

Yo me acuerdo de Avelino. Me acuerdo tamién de los tres hermanos, pero más me acuerdo de Avelino. Él estaba mal del sentido, y cuando quedó de huérfano, quedó de mendigo ahi en Cabezón. Quedó con esta señora Petra, y luego se jueron ella y su familia pa Selima [Seligman], y se quedó Avelino en Cabezón.

Avelino cuando llegaba a casa, que era seguido, le dicía a mamá "hermana." A papá hermano. Vinía y agarraba l'hacha y se ponía a partir leña y loo lo llamaba mamá y le daba comida.

—¡Ya está güeno Avelino! ¡Vente a comer!

—Güeno hermana. Güeno.

Pero [lo] más que me acuerdo yo de Avelino es que él se metía en una ramada y se quedaba dormido. Era del dijunto Ricardo [Heller] que tenía tienda. Un día pasamos un bonche de plebe por un lao de la ramada onde estaba Avelino atrás del corral y salió tirándonos pedradas. Por tanto me da a mí que a mi hermano. Nosotros estábanos chicos. Estaba mal del sentido. Yo me solté llorando. Y loo me dijo:

—¡Vente m' hijito! Tú eres hijo de mi hermano. ¡Esos mendigos! ¡Esos mendigos!—dijo—. ¡Juan Disco de la calle!

Dijía Avelino:

—Ustedes [él y su hermano] son hijos de mi hermano. Ustedes son hijitos de mi hermano. ¡Váyanse pa la casa! ¡Váyanse ustedes! ¡Esos mendigos!

Como no nos da un peñascazo. ¡Ay qué susto llevé yo! Pero siempre me acordaré de lo que hizo por consolarme. Estaría mal del sentido, pero Avelino en algunos modos tenía güen juicio.

STORIES

BENJAMÍN ("BENNY") LUCERO

Avelino

I remember Avelino. I also remember the three siblings, but I remember Avelino best. He was mentally retarded, and when he was left an orphan, he became a beggar there in Cabezón. He lived with a lady named Petra, but when she and her family moved to Seligman, Avelino stayed in Cabezón.

Avelino came to our house often, and he called my mother "Sister" and my father "Brother." He would grab the ax and chop wood until my mother would call for him to come and eat.

"That's enough, Avelino! Come and eat!"

"Okay, Sister. Okay."

What I recall most clearly about Avelino is that he used to go into a livestock shed and fall asleep. It was owned by Ricardo, Ricardo Heller, a local merchant. One day a bunch of us kids went by the shed and taunted Avelino, and he came out hurling rocks at us. He almost hit me as well as my brother. He was off his rocker. We were small. I started crying. Then he said to me:

"Come here, my son. You are my brother's son. Those kids are nothing but beggars! Beggars! Good-for-nothings!"

Avelino kept repeating:

"You [he and his brother] are sons of my brother. Go home! Go, go! Those beggars!"

Little wonder he didn't crack our heads. Boy, was I scared, but I'll always remember how he tried to comfort me. Perhaps Avelino was mentally retarded, but in some ways he was very human.

BENJAMÍN ("BENNY") LUCERO

Con un'hacha lo mataron

Conforme me platicaba mi papá [Clemente Lucero], un celo jue la muerte de Juan Valdez. Creo que por una mujer. Y tamién una vez tuvo Juan Valdez un pleito con este Emiliano Sandoval,[1] por puros chismes, yo creo. Resultaba que jueron compadres, pero una vez le pegó el dijunto Juan bien a bien a este Emiliano.

Cuando la muerte, Emiliano Sandoval traiba un compañero.[2] Entiendo que era Molina. En una vez había ido Molina a pidir esta muchacha soltera y no quiso casarse con él. Tengo entendido que la muchacha quería más a Juan Valdez, y por ahi le agarró mala voluntá este Molina[3] al dijunto Juan Valdez.

El dijunto Juan Valdez tenía tres hijos: una muchita que dormía con él, y dos muchitos. Uno de ellos estaba medio mal del mente. Se llamaba Avelino.[4] Juan Valdez tenía güen atajo de vacas y muncha caballada y mulas. Una vez, cuando él jue a buscar sus mulas, Molina y Sandoval se toparon con él y lo embolaron. Andaban en pues de él. Le tenían mala pica. Cuando Juan Valdez regresó patrás pa la casa, llegó embolao. Se acostó en la cama con su hijita. Ai entraron y le pegaron Emiliano y Molina. Con un'hacha lo mataron.

Avelino le dijo a mi papá:

—Mira hermano, Emiliano le dio a en papá con l'hacha, y luego le dio con l'hacha el Molina este.

Esque le dijo Emiliano, "dale tú tamién."

—¡Luego pegó la sangre al techo!—dijo Avelino. A nosotros, a mis hermanitos y a mí, nos pusieron la pistola pa que nos tapáranos la cabeza, pa que no viéranos, pero jue Emiliano el que lo mató. Yo lo vide. Primero le dio Emiliano a en papá con l'hacha y loo le dio el otro, Molina. Con una hacha lo mataron.

Platicaba en papá que loo de ahi sacaron al dijunto Juan Valdez y con el cabresto amarrao en la cabeza de la silla del

BENJAMÍN ("BENNY") LUCERO

They Murdered Him with an Ax

According to my father, Clemente Lucero, jealousy was the cause of Juan Valdez's death. You see, once Juan Valdez had a disagreement with Emiliano Sandoval,[1] all because of some gossip. Even though Juan and Emiliano were coparents, Juan once beat the tar out of Emiliano.

At the time of Juan Valdez's death, Emiliano Sandoval had a companion with him, and I understand it was Molina.[2] Molina had once asked for a young girl's hand in marriage, and she refused to marry him. Apparently, the girl liked Juan Valdez more, and ever since then, Molina[3] disliked Juan Valdez.

The late Juan Valdez was the father of three children: a little girl, who used to sleep with him, and two boys. One of them was a bit off his rocker. His name was Avelino.[4] Juan Valdez had a good herd of cattle and many horses and mules. One time, when Juan went to look for his mules, Molina and Sandoval found him and got him drunk. They were really out to get him; they had it in for him. Juan returned home drunk and fell asleep in the bed where his daughter was sleeping. That's where he was when Emiliano and Molina hit him. They killed him with an ax.

Avelino told my father, "Look brother, Emiliano hit my dad with ax, and then he gave the ax to Molina and told Molina to hit him. Then the blood hit the ceiling! They aimed a pistol at my small brother and sister and me so we would cover our heads and not be able to witness anything, but it was Emiliano who killed him. I saw it. Emiliano was the first one to hit my dad with the ax, and then Molina took his turn. They murdered him with an ax."

My father said that afterward they took Juan's body out of the house, and with a rope tied to the saddle horn, they dragged him and dumped him in a small creek. There they covered him with an embankment; it was so heavy it made him have a bowel movement.

caballo, lo arrastraron y lo tiraron en el arroyito este. Ahi en el arroyo le echaron un barranco, que estaba tan pesao que cuando cayó arriba dél pasó el cuerpo.

En papá, como te estoy dijiendo, había venido d'en casa a la estafeta ahi en Cabezón.[5] Él había visto unos caballos; uno d'ellos, de Emiliano o de Molina, estaba herrao.

Y fíjate tú, al dijunto Emiliano por pura política lo nombraron al jurao. Güeno, el caso es que cuando el jurao jue a Cabezón a envestigar, don Emiliano estaba aferrao en cierta juella:

—Ésta no es la juella de los caballos—dijía. —Ésta no es la juella de los caballos.

Quería él limpiarse que no era la juella del caballo que iba herrao. Pero el jurao se afirmó a siguir la juella de los caballos. Jueron hasta el mero corral, ai en el Cabezón. Porque ellos [la familia Valdez] vivían abajo, al sur del Cabezón, al sur poniente.

Más tarde arrestaron las autoridades a Emiliano y a Molina y echaron juera del jurao a Emiliano. Y ahi cuando lo jueron persicutando, pus, lo quebraron. Era dueño de munchas borregas y de tienda en el Cabezón donde tenía estafeta este [E]miliano Sandoval. Quedó sin nada. No se quedó más de con el tiro de caballos y el bogue conque abandonó ese pais, junto con su mamá y la mujer, pero lo soltaron libre. Faltaron pruebas. Tamién a Molina, asegún tengo entendido.

Tamién después platicaba en papá que esque este hombre Molina andaba ahi en el Cabezón y pa ondequiera que andaba, andaba hecho rifle en el caballo. Y iba mi papá una vez "Y lo siguí yo," dijo. "Traiba una mula ensillada este Molina. Lo siguí," dijo. "Y me tendí y le jalé el rifle. Le quité el rifle." Ya esque abría tamaños ojos el viejo ese. "Yo tenía tamién coraje," dijo en papá, "porque sabía que él era el que había matao a mi padrino, pero yo me tendí en la mula y le agarré el rifle. Después se lo entregué; no se lo debía haber entregao."

My father had gone from our house to the post office in Cabezón.[5] There he had seen these horses and noticed that one of them was shod. So either Emiliano Sandoval or Molina's horse was shod.

"And imagine this," my father said. "Emiliano was selected for the jury just because of his political connections. The fact is that when the jury went to Cabezón to investigate, Don Emiliano was bent on a certain trail."

"This isn't the horses' trail," he said. "This is not the horses' trail."

He wanted to wash his hands of the whole matter, saying that it wasn't the trail of the shod horse. But the jury insisted on following the trails. They went right up to the corral there in Cabezón, just south-southwest of where the Valdez family lived.

Later, Emiliano was thrown off the jury and he and Molina were arrested. In the end, the jury broke Emiliano, but they freed him for lack of evidence. Emiliano had once owned in Cabezón many sheep and a store, where he had a post office, but he went broke. The only thing he had left was a team of horses and a buggy that he used to get away from that country, his mother, and his wife. They also dropped charges against Molina.

My father said that Molina rode around Cabezón, and everywhere he went, he carried a rifle on his horse. Once when my father was on his way somewhere, he followed Molina.

"I followed him," he said. "And I snuck up on him and took his rifle away. This made the old man open his eyes wide! I was really upset because I knew very well that he was one of the ones who had killed my godfather. That's why I snuck up on him and took away his rifle. Later I gave it back to him; I shouldn't have given it back to him.

"As for me," said my father, "Emiliano used to treat me very well." My father and Emiliano were good buddies. Because my father spoke Navajo quite well, he interpreted for Emiliano when he was collecting money from the Navajos; but Juan Valdez was also my father's godfather."

"A mí me trataba muy bien [E]miliano," dijía en papá.
Porque él [el papá de Benny Lucero] y Emiliano anduvieron
muncho juntos. Esque en papá hablaba muncho el navajó, y
anduvo de intérpete de Emiliano allá por los navajoses, coletando
dinero y trabajó por él, pero Juan Valdez tamién era padrino d'en
papá.

De Albuquerque se jue pal Paso este Sandoval. Y el otro,
Molina, tamién no sé que le pasó. Eran tres los que andaban, pero
dos d'ellos jueron los que con un'hacha lo mataron a este Juan
Valdez ahi en Cabezón. No, no lo penitensaron. Pero mira. Dijía
en papá que "Dios no castiga con palos ni azotes."

SIFREDO ROMERO

Lo que pierdo aquí, lo gano allá

Una vez estaba trabajando con un hombre ahi en Casa Salazar,
y se quejó que estaba lloviendo. Ya tenía dos, tres días que estaba lloviendo.

—¿Y est' agua qué viene a molestar?—dijo—. No deja trabajar.

No faltó quién abriera la boca.

—¡Mira! Sifredo se está riyendo.

—¿Por qué?—dijo el hombre.

—Porque le gusta la lluvia. Él quiere que llueva.

Voltió así y me vido. Me dijo:

—¿Qué tú quieres que llueva?

—Sí señor—le dije.

Y me dijo:

—¿Por qué? Te vas a perder el día de hoy.

—Si lo pierdo no le hace—le dije—. Lo que pierdo aquí, lo
gano allá. Lo va a ganar usté tamién—le dije.

From Albuquerque this Sandoval went to El Paso. As for Molina, I don't know what became of him. There were three of them but only two were responsible for delivering the fatal blow to Juan Valdez in Cabezón. Neither Emiliano nor Molina ever went to prison for this crime, but as my father used to say, "God doesn't punish with sticks or beatings."

SIFREDO ROMERO

Whatever I Lose Here, I'll Gain Down the Road

Once I was working with a man in Casa Salazar, and he complained because it was raining. It had been raining for two or three days.

"What business does this rain have bothering us?" asked the man. "It doesn't let you work."

Then someone said, "Look! Sifredo is laughing."

"Why?" asked the man.

"Because he is enjoying the rain. He wants it to rain!"

So the man who had complained turned, looked at me, and asked, "Do you want it to rain?"

"Yes, sir," I replied.

He quickly countered, "Why? You are going to lose today's work."

"If I lose it, it doesn't matter," I replied. "Whatever I lose here, I'll gain down the road. You're going to profit as well."

"How so?" he queried.

"If the farmer can't raise crops," I said, "how's the merchant going to have food to sell to you? Doesn't the merchant's food supply come from the farmer? Doesn't the farmer rely on the rain to raise his crops?"

"Yes," he said. "Well, let it rain then!"

"Let it rain!" added Sifredo (laughter).

—¿*Por qué?*—*dijo.*

—*Pus si el ranchero no levanta*—*le dije yo*—, ¿*diónde le va vender el comerciante a usté?* ¿*Qué no viene del ranchero la comida pal comerciante?* ¿*Qué no se atiene el ranchero de la lluvia pa la cosecha?*

—*Sí*—*dijo*—. ¡*Pues antonces que llueva!*

—¡*Pus que llueva!*—*dijo Sifredo (risas).*

Teodoro García

Dios nos dio su bendición bendita

Cuando ya nosotros nos casamos, mi compañera y yo procuramos a criar a nuestra familia y trabajar del modo que se pudiera arquerir el pan de cada día. Vivíanos en Casa Salazar, pero había en el Cabezón un comercio de don Ricardo Heller. Yo no sé qué nación sería, pero muy güen hombre. Y allá iba yo por la comida que necitábanos.

Yo era fletero de Ricardo Heller. Yo acarriaba carga dél y de otros pal Alburquerque, y de aquí la llevábanos al Cabezón en carro de caballos. Nos tardábanos cinco, seis días, en ida y vuelta. Cuando venía el tiempo de que los navajoses tresquilaban sus borregas, empacaban la lana, se la llevaban a Ricardo, y yo la fletiaba en los carros pa Alburquerque. Los navajoses le traiban cabras o vacas o lo que sea a Ricardo, y me las despachaba a mí pa que criara yo al partido lo mismo de cabras que de vacas.

Ricardo jue un hombre muy güeno conmigo y mi compañera; estábanos recién casaos. Nosotros criamos munchas vacas, muchas cabras, y munchos caballos después que nos casamos, y cosechamos muncho tamién. Casi puedo decir que

TEODORO GARCÍA

God Gave Us His Holy Blessing

After we got married, my wife and I worked hard to earn our daily bread and raise our family. We lived in Casa Salazar, but there was in Cabezón a trading post that belonged to Don Ricardo Heller. I don't know his nationality, but he was a good man. It was at his trading post that I bought what food we did not grow.

I was a freighter for Ricardo Heller. I hauled his and others' cargo to Albuquerque and back in my wagon. Coming and going, the trip took us five, sometimes six days. When the Navajos sheared their sheep, they took the fleece to Ricardo, and I freighted the wool to Albuquerque. The Navajos brought to Ricardo goats and cows as well, and he would turn all of them over to me to raise.

Ricardo was very good to me and my wife; we were newlyweds, just starting out. By raising so much livestock and by growing so much corn and wheat crops, we became the mainstays in our area. We raised up to twenty hogs, and we used them for both eating and selling. We used to plant a lot of corn and wheat. When the wheat ripened and was ready for harvest, I'd gather ten, fifteen, twenty men to cut it and stack it. Then I'd thresh it with mares in a threshing field that was so well prepared no wheat was lost. Many people poorer than we were helped themselves to flour, bread, corn, and wheat at our house. People took care of their basic food needs at our home.

For a long time, the countryside was available for raising cows, goats, horses—everything. The government didn't prohibit us from doing that until it passed a law reducing our grazing rights. Then we weren't able to raise very many animals. Of course, we paid rent only for the land we did use, but the government showed no mercy or gratitude. I don't know if what the government did to us was fair or not. Only God knows that. The

éranos como los principales del lugar. Criábanos hasta veinte cochinos; tenía pal uso de vender y comer. Yo y mi compañera sembrábanos muncho maiz, muncho trigo. Cuando venía el tiempo que el trigo se maduraba, yo juntaba diez, quince, veinte hombres pa cortar el trigo pa pilalo. Loo lo trillaba con yeguas en un era hecha, tan bien hecha que no se perdiera nada. Y la gente más pobre que nosotros, de ahí llevaban harina, llevaban pan, maiz, y trigo. La gente se suplía de sus necesidades ahí en casa.

Por un largo tiempo teníanos libre el campo pa andar y pa criar vacas, cabras, caballos y todo. No nos privó el gobierno hasta que vino que pasaron una ley que nos redujo. Pagábanos renta por el terreno que pisábanos, pero el gobierno jue muy ingrato con nosotros. Yo no sé si sería justo o injusto el gobierno lo que hizo con nosotros. Eso sólo Dios sabe. Los hombres ricos arrentaron los mejores pasteos, pero la gente probe no podía por la proveza. Había gente muy probe y tenía que vivir con la siembrita y con su inteligencia.

Porque nosotros cuando nos casamos, éranos muy probes porque yo quedé solo en el mundo, y mi compañera tamién. Pero gracias a Dios y su bendición, criamos munchas vacas, cabras, caballos, y cosechamos muncho. Yo me recuerdo, y me recordaré hasta que me muera, en mi Dios que nos ayudó muncho. Dios nos dio su bendición bendita.

wealthy rented the best pasturelands, but the poor people in the valley couldn't afford to do this. They were poor and had to survive on their small crops and by their wits.

Here we were, just married and very poor, because I was left an orphan, and so was my mate, but thanks to God's will and God's blessing, we raised many cows, goats, horses, and crops. I recall, and I'll do so until the day I die, that God helped us a lot. God gave us His holy blessing.

Notes

1. Emiliano Sandoval at one time was sheriff of Sandoval County and allegedly exerted considerable political influence throughout the county, including the Río Puerco Valley.

2. Newspaper accounts as well as information from old-timers who have been interviewed claim that there were at least two and possibly three men with Emiliano Sandoval the night of the murder.

3. Molina (no first name was given) is not a name mentioned by some of the interviewees who have talked to me about the murder of Juan Valdez.

4. Avelino, the oldest of the siblings, was about fifteen years old at the time his father was murdered, but, since he was mentally retarded, his testimony before the grand jury was disallowed. His siblings were minors and also could not testify.

5. Prior to the death of Juan Valdez, Emiliano Sandoval was the postmaster of Cabezón. Evidently, monies had been missing from the post office account and Valdez knew who the perpetrator was in the community. According to Bencés Gabaldón, one of my interviewees, "The only reason this man [Juan Valdez] was murdered is because he knew that this fellow by the name of Emiliano Sandoval had robbed the post office. This fellow ran the post office and one day money was missing from it." Nasario García, *Recuerdos de los viejitos: Tales of the Río Puerco* (Albuquerque: University of New Mexico Press, 1987).

GALO GARCÍA, SON OF ANTONIO
PADILLA GARCÍA AND TAIDA
SÁNCHEZ-GARCÍA, IN GUADALUPE,
N.M., C. 1942. PHOTO COURTESY
OF THE AUTHOR.

JUAN JARAMILLO (1870?–1939),
SHEEPHERDER AND SONGSMITH, IN
SAN LUIS, N.M., C. 1922–24. PHOTO
COURTESY OF EDUMENIO LOVATO.

CHAPTER 4

CORRIDOS

BALLADS

Bᴀʟʟᴀᴅs, ʟɪᴋᴇ ʀɪᴅᴅʟᴇs, ʜᴀᴠᴇ ʙᴇᴇɴ ᴀɴ ɪɴᴛᴇɢʀᴀʟ ᴘᴀʀᴛ ᴏꜰ ᴛʜᴇ Hɪsᴘᴀɴɪᴄ oral tradition in the Southwest since colonial times. In Mexico, as elsewhere in the Southwest and New Mexico, they are known as corridos and are sung, not recited, as was sometimes true of the Spanish *romance*, or ballad. Nevetheless, the link between Spain and Mexico is undeniable. The eminent Mexican scholar Vicente T. Mendoza wrote in *El romance español y el corrido mexicano* (Mexico: Imprenta Universitaria, 1939), "When the Spanish conquistadors landed on our shores, they brought with them the *romance*." The appeal of the romance could not be kept in check; it spread like wildfire. Mendoza also affirms the separation of the

Mexican ballad from the Spanish romance, but he also underscores the fact that the corrido could now stand alone. The first work in Mexico resembling a corrido, according to Mendoza, is *Coplas al Tapado* (1684). At the beginning of the nineteenth century, Higinio Vázquez Santana published *Corrido de Carlos IV*, and other corridos followed. Since its inception, the ballad has enjoyed a widespread popularity in Mexico. In fact, one cannot visit Mexico today without hearing a corrido on the radio or on television. This popularity extends well into the southwestern United States, especially in New Mexico.

The corrido, like the Spanish romance, is a song that is narrative in form, with eight- or sixteen-syllable verses in assonated rhyme. Corridos were typically written by an anonymous *poeta* (or *pueta*, in small New Mexico communities) and were of a popular nature. Their themes include unrequited love, personal tragedy, man's inhumanity to man, patriotism, assassinations and murders, disobedience, and a host of other topics. In rare cases, the ballads have an implicit didactic function, but their main purpose was to tell a story, not to moralize.

The singing of the corrido could be simple or complex. It could be sung by just one musician, who typically played a guitar, or by an entire group, such as a *mariachi*, band, with many musicians playing a variety of wind and string instruments. The instrument commonly used first in the New World, and in Mexico in particular, was the *vihuela española*. A small guitar, it was popular beginning in the sixteenth century until it was replaced by the Spanish guitar. Later the mandolin and harp appeared and became popular. As the corrido gained in popularity, the number of instruments grew, as did the number of women singers.

Among a corrido's identifying characteristics are its sense of joyfulness and playfulness. It is at once restless and quiet, and it has a kind of fluidity that enables it to glide (*correr*) without interruption. Since older ballads in the Southwest are part of the oral heritage, the chances of their disappearing are great. Nevertheless, their appeal is remarkable, perhaps due to their plain and unadulterated language, which is devoid of metaphors or symbols. Their simplicity makes them accessible to all.

The corridos presented here are arranged thematically and thus lead the reader on a journey that runs from the romantic to the tragic to the humorous. One fascinating feature of these corridos is that they feature events that were of interest to the local people. This is especially true of the ballads "Corrido de Juan Valdez," written in honor of Juan Valdez, who was brutally murdered with an ax in Cabezón in 1908, and of "Corrido de un vaquero," which is about Rafael, a cowboy from Cabezón, who was killed by a horse. Eduardo Valdez donated another ballad with the same title, and it presents a light and humorous view of a cowboy's life. One of the most beautiful ballads in this collection is "El huérfano," composed by a son who yearns for his parents' presence because he misses their advice and affection. "El hijo desobediente" is of Mexican origin, and it epitomizes the predictable yet tragic outcome of the headstrong son who, in the midst of a brawl with another young man about a woman, ignored his father's advice to refrain from fighting and is killed by his opponent. The theme of the disobedient son was quite well known among Hispanics in communities such as those of the Río Puerco Valley. At one time, every villager could recount a story or sing a corrido about a disobedient son who raised his right arm to his father or mother in a moment of rage only to have it disabled as punishment from God.

The composition of ballads in Hispanic communities in New Mexico is not a recent phenomenon, as the ensuing corridos will attest. Both World Wars, and the Korean and Vietnam wars thereafter, inspired ballads recording the tragic loss of sons, daughters, and friends. Similar events and other tragedies inspire the composition of such songs and hence continue the popularity of the corrido. Indeed, the corrido is one kind of Hispanic music that thrives in New Mexico and throughout the Southwest.

Corridos

Edumenio Lovato

Clavelito*

I

Clavelito, clavelito
No me dejes de querer
Eres rosa de castilla
Cortada al amanecer.

II

Tú serás la consentida **
Tú serás mi bienestar
Como Dios me dé licencia
Contigo me he de casar.

III

Clavelito, clavelito
No me dejes tú de amar
Eres ángel de mi guarda
Que me vas acompañar.

IV

Tú eres la consentida
Tú eres mi bienestar
Como Dios me dé licencia
Contigo me he de casar.

My Little Pink Carnation*

I

My little pink carnation
My little pink carnation
Don't stop loving me
You're my red rose
Picked at daybreak.

II

You shall be my favorite one **
You shall be my everything
Should God grant me
permission
I shall be the one to marry you.

III

My little pink carnation
My little pink carnation
Don't stop loving me
You're my guardian angel
Who's going to accompany me.

IV

You're my favorite one
You're my everything
Should God grant me
permission
I shall be the one to marry you.

---

* A ballad of Mexican provenance that Edumenio Lovato's paternal grandfather dictated to him when Edumenio was a boy.

** A Mexican term of endearment.

V

Clavelito, clavelito
Ven para decirte adiós
No me dejes ir solito
Vámonos juntos los dos.

VI

Tú serás la consentida
Tú serás mi bienestar
Como Dios me dé licencia
Contigo me he de casar.

V

My little pink carnation
My little pink carnation
Come so I can bid you
farewell
Don't let me go all alone
Let us both go together.

VI

You shall be my favorite one
You shall be my everything
Should God grant me
permission
I shall be the one to marry
you.

EDUMENIO LOVATO

El Corrido de Luisita

I

Adiós Cebolla* mentada
¿Por qué te muestras esquiva?
Los palos y piedras lloran
So de ver a Luisita cautiva.

II

Adiós querida Luisita
Lo qué te encargo has de hacer
Ya bajando a Granada
Los puños nos van hacer.

III

Bonito plan de La Villa
Donde se crió Luisita
Juan de Azul se la llevó
Porque era mujer bonita.

* A town in Mexico.

The Ballad of Luisita

I

Good-bye famous Cebolla*
Why are you so elusive?
Sticks and stones weep
Just by seeing Luisita captive.

II

Good-bye my dear Luisita
You must do as I [Juan de Azul] say
As you approach Granada
People will clench their fists at us.

III

Beautiful town of La Villa
Where Luisita grew up
Juan de Azul took her with him
Because she was a beautiful
woman.

IV

Juan de Azul tenía un caballo
Pistolas y su buena silla
Para llevarse a Luisita
Del mero plan de La Villa.

V

Su padre como era rico
Luego formó un batallón
Para agarrar a Juan de Azul
Porque era un hombre ladrón.

VI

Adiós querida Luisita
Adiós querida mujer
Se les concedió a tus padres
De ver mi sangre correr.

VII

Todas las estrellas dicen
Que solo tuve la culpa
De querer a quien no me quiera
Y de buscar a quien no me busca.

IV

Juan de Azul had a horse,
Pistols and a good saddle
So as to whisk Luisita away
From the very center of La Villa.

V

Since her father was rich
He quickly assembled a battalion
To capture Juan de Azul
Who was a thief.

VI

Good-bye my dear Luisita
Good-bye my dear lady
Your parents got their wish
Which was to see my [Juan de Azul's] blood flow.

VII

All of the stars attest
That I alone was to blame
For unrequited love and
For searching for someone fruitlessly.

EDUMENIO LOVATO

Corrido de Bernardo

I

Ayuda pido a Jesús
Y a La Reina Soberana
Voy a escribir una carta
De una muy notable fama.

The Ballad of Bernardo

I

I ask Jesus Christ for help
And the Sovereign Queen, too,
I'm going to write a letter
Concerning a very notable deed.

II

*Mató a un alcalde en
su tierra
Por una bastante causa
Y Bernardo por evitar
cuestión
Se fue a la Villa de Francia.*

III

*Donde él se enamoró
De una muy pulida dama
Bernarda tiene por nombre
Y él Bernardo se llamaba
Como eran de un propio
nombre
Mucho se querían y se
amaban.*

IV

*Ya sale el corrigidor
Y les impide la entrada
Al cual tumban, a cual matan
A cual cuerpo destrozaban
Ya matan al desposado
Y a los padres de esta niña
Y se llevan a Bernarda.*

V

*El más chico que iba guiando
Les dice aquí estas palabras:
—Amigos, hemos perdido
El lobo este en la embuscada.*

VI

*Más se sonríe Bernardo
Y de esta manera les habla:
—No teman al mundo entero
Ni otros mil mundos
que haigan*

II

He murdered a mayor in
his land
For a very good reason
And Bernardo, avoiding
conflict,
Left for a town in France.

III

There he fell in love
With a beautiful young lady
Bernarda is her name
And Bernardo was his name
Since both had identical names
They liked and loved one
another.

IV

The mayor presents himself
And blocks their entrance
They knock him down, and
kill him
and destroy his body.
They [mayor's men] are about
to kill the suitor [Bernardo]
As well as the girl's parents,
And they whisk away Bernarda.

V

The smallest man leading
Recites to them these words:
"Friends, we have lost
The wolf in the search."

VI

Bernardo smiles even more
And speaks to them in
this way:
"Don't fear the entire world

Que yo les desfenderé
A los cantos de mis pistolas
Y a los filos de mi espada.

VII

Ya salen las companías
De la refriega pasada
Matan a sus compañeras
Sólo Bernardo escapaba
Y vino una bala veloz
Que a su caballo le tumbaba
Luego que vieron caer
Le dieron cuatro estocadas
Y se llevaron a Bernarda.

VIII

Con sus delicados pies
Con sus delicadas plantas
Pisando la tierra dura
Pisando la tierra blanda.

IX

Voltea la cara Bernarda
Un punto que cerca estaba:
—¡Ay! Bernardo de mi vida
Más ¡Ay! Bernardo de
mi alma
Que corta fue mi partida
Y mi desdicha fue tanta.

X

Luego que se vido bueno
Bernardo para Portugués
ganaba
Donde estaba un capitán
"Brazos Fuertes" le llamaba
Y el capitán le agradece

Nor another one thousand
For I shall defend all of you
At the sound of my pistols
And the sharpness of my sword."

VII

The companies are departing
From the preceding scuffle
They've killed his [Bernardo's]
companions
Only Bernardo was able
to escape
And along came a fleeting bullet
That struck and fell his horse
As soon as they saw it fall
They followed with four
sword thrusts
And off they went with
Bernarda.

VIII

With her delicate feet
With the soles of her delicate feet
Stepping on the hard ground
Stepping on the soft ground.

IX

Bernarda turns her face
Indicating she was close by:
"Oh! My beloved Bernardo
But oh, my dear Bernardo
My, but my departure was brief
And my misfortune so
prolonged."

X

As soon as he was well
Bernardo headed for Portugal
Where there was a captain
"Strong Arms" was his name
And the captain thanks him

Y con arrogansa le habla
Le ofrecío un caballo blanco
Que al par de viento volaba.

XI

Salieron las companías
De la refriega pasada
A cual tumban, a cual matan
A cual cuerpo destrozaban
El único que escapó
Fue el de la yegua alazana
Si de ésa no se vale
A los demás acompaña.

XII

Aquí la tengo amiguita
Como una querida niña
Como una querida hermana
Que ya está de Dios
Mi gusto que será, que
se haga.

And speaks to him with
arrogance
He offered him a white horse
That would fly with the wind.

XI

The companies emerged
From the preceding scuffle
They knock down people here,
they kill people there
Destroying people in
the process.
The only one who managed
to escape
Was the rider [Bernarda] on
the sorrel mare
If she hadn't taken advantage of it
She would have been killed too.

XII

Here she is, my dear friend
Like a dear sweet girl
Like a beloved sister
Who now rests with God
Whatever may be, may be.

EDUMENIO LOVATO

El Quelite[1]

I

Que bonito es el Quelite
Bien haiga quien lo formó
Que por sus orillas tiene
De quién acordarme yo.

II

Mañana me voy, mañana
Mañana me voy de aquí
El consuelo que me queda
Que se han de acordar de mí.

El Quelite[1]

I

How lovely is El Quelite
Bless him who established it
Thanks to its outskirts
I'm able to remember it.

II

Tomorrow I depart, tomorrow
Tomorrow I'm leaving here
The consolation I retain
Is that they'll remember me.

III

Camino de San Ignacio[2]
Me dio sueño y me dormí
Y me despertó un gallito
Cantando, quiri, qui, qui.

IV

Cuando yo me vaya y vuelva
Si aún me quieres hablar
Si no has hallado amante
Volveremos a tratar.

V

Al pie de un limón muy verde
Me dio sueño y me dormí
*Y me despertó mi negra**
Diciendo—Ya estoy aquí.

VI

Muy contento me despido
Porque con mi amor volví
Ahora sólo les pido
Que se acuerden siempre
de mí.

*A term of endearment.

III

En route to San Ignacio[2]
I got sleepy and fell asleep
And a little rooster woke me up
Crowing cock-a-doodle-doo.

IV

After I've gone and come back
If you still want to talk to me
If you haven't found a lover
We shall try once again.

V

At the foot of a green lemon tree
I got sleepy and fell asleep
And my sweetheart woke me up
Saying to me, "I'm back again."

VI

I take leave very happy
Because I'm back with my love
Now all I ask of you
Is always to remember me.

EDUMENIO LOVATO

¡Qué bonita es mi casita!

How Beautiful Is My House!

I

¡Qué bonita es mi casita!
Allí todo es un primor
Nada más que está solita
Porque le falta su amor.

I

How beautiful is my house!
Everything in it is beautiful
The only thing is she's all alone
Because she is missing her love.

II

Si quieres vamos a Puebla[3]
Corresponde a mi pasión
Hasta allá amor dividido
Dueño de mi corazón.

III

Al llegar el tren de Puebla
Nos vamos a la estación
En la nueva carretera[4]
Nos vamos en camión.

IV

Al llegar a mi casita
Verás que alegre mansión
Una cotorra mancita
Y un perrito juguetón.

V

Un altar con muchas flores
En frente se ve al pasar
Con cortinas y colores
Que adornan aquel lugar.

VI

En este altar me acompañan
Y me dan su bendición
La Virgen Guadalupana[5]
Y Sagrado Corazón.

VII

Una máquina, un armario
Una cama en un rincón
Una elétrica pantalla[6]
Que alumbra mi habitación.

VIII

Un fonógrafo[7] *excelente*
Que alegre mi corazón
Una guitarra colgada
Con sus liras de listón.

II

If you wish let's go to Puebla[3]
That is in keeping with
my passion
Until there our love is fragmented
Keeper of my own heart.

III

When the train arrives
from Puebla
We will go to the railroad station
On the new highway[4]
We will travel on a bus.

IV

As we get to my little house
You'll see a joyful mansion
And a tame little parrot
And a playful little dog.

V

An altar with many flowers
Can be seen as one passes by
With different color drapes
That adorn this place.

VI

On this altar they join me
And they give me their blessing
The Virgin of Guadalupe[5]
As well as the Sacred Heart.

VII

A sewing machine, a closet
And a bed in a corner
A movie screen[6]
Which illuminates my room.

VIII

An excellent phonograph[7]
How happy my heart is
A guitar hanging
With its ribbon strings.

IX

Dos espejitos franceses
Y cuadros alrededor
Mil adornos japoneses
Un reloj despertador.

X

A mi casita bonita
No más le falta el calor
Si quieres, vamos, chiquita
Allí crecerá nuestro amor.

IX

Two small French mirrors
And pictures all around them
A thousand Japanese
knickknacks
And an alarm clock.

X

My small beautiful house
All it's lacking is warmth
If you wish my sweetheart
There our love shall grow.

EDUMENIO LOVATO

Los cazadores*

The Trappers*

I

Novecientos veinte y cuatro
Les haré saber señores
*Velarde y Gabaldón***
Se meten de cazadores.

II

Ya destendieron sus trampas
Por toditos los cañones
No agarran ni pajaritos.
Ni conejos ni ratones.

III

Pues Erminio Gabaldón
Un joven de las primeras
Manda por una troca
Y es para llevar los cueros.

I

Nineteen-hundred-twenty-four
I'll let all of you know
Velarde and Gabaldón**
Decide to become trappers.

II

They've already set their traps
Throughout all of the canyons
But they can't even catch
tiny birds.
Nor rabbits or mice.

III

Erminio Gabaldón,
An upright young man,
Sends for a truck
To pick up the hides.

*A New Mexican ballad.
**Persons' names are New Mexican rather than Mexican.

IV

Dice Antonio Velarde
A don Macario Lobato
—Nos está illendo muy bien
Pues ya agarramos un gato.

V

—El dinero que me toque
Voy a ponerlo en el banco
Ése será para mi hijito
No quiero dejarlo en blanco.

VI

Vienen en su embolancita
Al paso y al medio trote
Pues ya agarramos dos gatos
Y de buena suerte un coyote.

VII

Dice Antonio Velarde
A Erminio Gabaldón
—El lonche no nos
cuesta nada
Lo agarramos de amontón

VIII

Fuerte está esta companía
A que bien ha progresado
Pues ya van embarcar
los cuervos
Para Denver, Colorado.

IX

Pues qué les dirá Erminio
Cuando su parte reciba
Yo haciendo el lonche
Y Antonio boca arriba.

X

Erminio tiene vergüenza
Ya no hallaba qué hacer

IV

Says Antonio Velarde
To Don Macario Lobato
"We're doing quite all right
Why, we've already caught a
bobcat."

V

"The money I've got coming
I'm going to put it in the bank
It'll be for my little son
I don't want to leave him
penniless."

VI

There they come in their buggy
At a trot and a gait
Why, we've already caught
two bobcats
And by chance a coyote as well.

VII

Says Antonio Velarde
To Erminio Gabaldón
"Lunch doesn't cost us anything
It comes to us hand over fist."

VIII

Strong is this company
Oh, how well it's progressed
Why the crows are headed
For Denver, Colorado.

IX

What will Erminio tell them
When he receives his share
Here I am preparing lunch
And Antonio is taking it easy.

X

Erminio is embarrassed
He was beside himself

Antonio boca arriba
Leyéndole el papel:
—Tú no sabes lo que pasa
Porque tú no sabes leer.

XI

Don Antonio Velarde
Quiere seguir la cazada
Este invierno venidero
A la zorra colorada
Erminio para que le haga el
lonche
Y él con la pierna cruzada.

XII

La fábrica de Colorado
Escribe con atención
—Afamados cazadores
Velarde y Gabaldón

XIII

Don Antonio Velarde
A Erminio le decía:
—Si agarramos hembra y
macho
Vamos hacer buena cría
Mientras seas buen muchacho
Siguiremos en companía.

XIV

Se apartó esta companía.
Haciendo partes iguales
Uno se fue para los toros
Y el otro para los primales.

XV

El que compuso estos versos
No ha sido compositor
Su nombre es Juan Jaramillo

Antonio taking it easy
Reading the newspaper to him
[Erminio]:
"You don't know what's happening
Because you don't know how
to read."

XI

Don Antonio Velarde
Wants to continue hunting
This coming winter
The reddish fox
So Erminio will fix him lunch
While he [Antonio] takes it easy.

XII

The Colorado factory
Writes very carefully
"Dear esteemed trappers
Velarde and Gabaldón."

XIII

Don Antonio Velarde
Says to Erminio:
"If we catch male and female
We're going to have a nice litter
As long as you're a good boy
We'll continue as partners."

XIV

The two of them parted
Dividing everything equally
One went to care for bulls
And the other became a sheep-
herder.

XV

He who composed these verses
Has not been a composer
His name is Juan Jaramillo

Para explicarles mejor	So you'll understand better
Si he tenido alguna falta	If I've erred in something
Dispénsemen* por favor.	Please forgive me for it.

*A Common New Mexico/Colorado metathesis of *dispénsenme.*

EDUMENIO LOVATO

El huérfano

I

Pues yo siento y me confundo
Es muy cierto y muy notable
La grande desdicha en
el mundo
No tener uno a sus padres.

II

Como la pluma en el aire
Anda el hijo ya perdido
El huérfano desvalido
Pierde el alma y el descoro
Escúchenme mis amigos
Estas lágrimas que lloro.

III

Estas lágrimas que lloro
No las lloro por cobarde
Las lloro porque me acuerdo
Los consejos de mi madre.

IV

Recuerdo los tristes días
Que cuando yo me pasaba
Mi madre por mí lloraba
Mi madre me bendecía.

The Orphan

I

I feel and am confused
It is very certain and
quite notable
That great misfortune in
this world
Is not to have one's parents.

II

Like a feather in the wind
The son walks around lost
The destitute orphan
Loses his soul and his honor.
Listen to me my friends
These tears that I shed.

III

These tears that I shed
Are not from being a coward
I shed them because I recall
The advice my mother gave me.

IV

I recall the sad days
When I roamed about
My mother cried for me
My mother would bless me.

V

Porque desgracia la mía
Sordo acabo en un momento
No tengo hora de contento
Vida mía tú bien lo sabes
Causa mucho sentimiento
No tener uno a sus padres.

VI

Unas veces [yo] de soldado
Otras veces en prisiones
Mi padre atribulado
Mi madre con aflicciones
Me llenaban de oraciones.

VII

Y mi madre el alma mía
Lloraba por mí en la calle
Así mi suerte sería.
¡Hay si vivieran mis padres!

VIII

Malos ratos y sonrojos
Mi madre por mí pasaba
Con lágrimas de sus ojos
Muchos consejos me daba.

IX

El vivir en el mundo
Para mí es desagradable
He quedado número uno
Con haber muerto mis padres.

X

Soy un hijo desgraciado
Amigos es la verdad
Porque Dios lo ha decretado
Que se haga su voluntad.

V

Why do I suffer so
I fall victim to silence
I don't have a happy moment
My dear mother you know
very well,
It causes a lot of grief
Not having one's parents.

VI

At times I am as a soldier
Other times I am imprisoned
My father, full of tribulation,
My mother, with afflictions,
Both showered me with blessings.

VII

And mother, the soul of my heart,
Used to weep for me in the street
That's how my fortune should be
If only my parents were still alive!

VIII

Embarrassing and shameful
moments
My mother suffered for me
With tears in her eyes
She gave me a lot of advice.

IX

Living in this world
Is unpleasant for me
I've been left alone
With my parents being gone.

X

I'm an unfortunate son
My friends, it's the truth
Because God has decreed it
May His will take its course.

XI

Lloraré como huérfano
que soy
Estos lamentos que doy
Son recuerdos de mis padres
Diré—¡Ay si viviera
mi madre!

XII

Pobrecita de mi madre
Con que lástima murió
Ahora sí ya se quedó
En el sueño más profundo
Pero desgraciado yo
Que quedé sólo en el mundo.

XIII

El que es huérfano señores
De todo el mundo sufre
desaire
Todos lo menosprecian
Porque no tiene a sus padres.

XIV

Para huérfano no hay sol
No hay cariño, no hay amores
Todos le hacen mala cara
Desprecian sus favores.

XV

Los tíos, parientes,
y conocidos
De todos modos lo desprecian
Dondequiera que
lo encuentran
De todos modos
lo avergüenzan.

XI

I'll cry like the orphan that I am
These moans that I let out
They are but my parents' memories I'll say again, "If only my
mother were alive!"

XII

My poor unfortunate mother
She died with such compassion
Now she's gone forever
In the profoundest sleep
But poor unfortunate me
Who's been left all alone in
this world.

XIII

He who's an orphan my friends
Suffers disdain from everyone
Everybody scorns him
Because he has no parents.

XIV

For the orphan there is no sun
There is no affection or love
Everyone turns the other way
They scorn his friendly gestures.

XV

Aunts, uncles, relatives,
and friends
No matter what, they're scornful
Wherever they run into him
No matter what, they
embarrass him.

XVI

Cantaba un preso una tarde
Una muy triste canción
Si mis padres vivieran
No me hallara yo en prisión
Estuvieran ellos en mi
presencia
Y me echarían su bendición

XVII

Hoy me encuentro aquí
encerrado
Sólo al Gran Supremo imploro
Soy un preso desgraciado
Para mí no hay tesoro.

XVIII

A hijos que tienen a sus padres
Un consejo yo les doy
Que respeten y amen a
sus padres
Para que no estén donde
yo estoy.

XIX

Para el huérfano señores
No hay cariño, no hay amores
Todo lo que recibe de otros
Son muchas penas y dolores.

XX

Aquí se acaba mi canción
Y a todos les deseo buena
suerte
Que mi único deseo para mí
Es que me visite la muerte.

XVI

One afternoon a prisoner sang
A very melancholy song
If only my parents were alive
I wouldn't find myself in prison
They'd both be at my side
And they would bless me.

XVII

Today I find myself locked up
I implore only the
Supreme Being
I'm an unfortunate prisoner
For me there is no treasure.

XVIII

To those who have their parents
I'll give you this advice
Respect and love your parents
So that you won't end up like me.

XIX

For the orphan, my friends,
There is no affection or love
What he receives from others
Is nothing more than pain
and grief.

XX

Here is where my song ends
And I wish everyone good luck
For the only wish I have
Is for death to come visit me.

EDUMENIO LOVATO

El hijo desobediente [8]

I

Un día estando herrando
Se encontraron dos varones
Metiendo mano a sus espadas
Más feroz que dos liones.

II

Calmado le dice uno al otro:
—No tenemos razón de peliar
Con buenas palabras los dos
Nos podemos arreglar.

III

Le responde el otro con ira:
—Yo no me someto arreglar
Hoy te prometo y te juro
Que la vida te ha de quitar.

IV

Dios nos dio nuestra vida
Para vivirla y gozarla
Y nadie tiene el derecho
A su prójimo quitarla.

V

La riña de estos jóvenes
A nadie le hicieron saber
Pero otros la sospechaban
Que la causa era una mujer.

VI

La ira y el celo juntos
Hacen muy mala
combinación
Se ciega el que los posea
Y pierde su buena razón.

The Disobedient Son [8]

I

One day as they were branding
Two young fellows found
themselves
Going for their swords
More ferociously than two lions.

II

Calmly one says to the other:
"We have no reason to fight
With a sensible exchange of words
The two of us can settle
the matter.

III

The other answered enraged:
"I don't yield to settlements
Today I promise and swear to you
That I'm going to put an end
to you."

IV

God gave us this life
To live and to enjoy
And no one has the right
To take it away from his neighbor.

V

The squabble between
these chaps
They informed no one of it
But others had their suspicion
That a woman was the cause of it.

VI

Rage and jealousy together
Make a very bad combination
He who is blinded by them
Loses his good senses.

VII

La ira y el mal intento
Es una cosa muy terrible
Querer quitar la vida a otro
Es un acto muy horrible.

VIII

Muchas veces esto pasa
Cuando el hombre comienza
a querer
Hay veces que hasta la
vida pierde
Por los celos por una mujer.

IX

El amor de la mujer es mentira
Sus cariños también
mentira son
Con mentiras ella engaña
al hombre
Y con mentiras le roba
el corazón.

X

Uno de ellos con ira peliaba
Para no dejar a su
adversario vivir
El otro con aguilez
se desfendía
Porque él no quería morir.

XI

Aunque los dos eran buenos
Para peliar con la espada
Por un tiempo los dos
Ni uno al otro se hacía nada.

XII

En fin llegó el momento
Cuando los dos luchaban
Su sangre empezó a correr
De las cortadas que se daban.

VII

Rage and bad intentions
Are a very terrible thing
To want to take someone
else's life
It's a very horrible act.

VIII

Many times that's what happens
When a man starts to love
There are times he even loses
his life
Just because of jealousy for
a woman.

IX

A woman's love is a falsehood
Her affection is also a lie
She deceives a man with
falsehoods
And with lies, steals his heart.

X

One of them fought with anger
So as not to let his enemy live
The other defended himself
with agility
Because he didn't want to die.

XI

Even though both were good
At fighting with their swords
For a while neither one of them
Inflicted any harm on the other.

XII

Finally the moment arrived
When both started struggling
Their blood started running
From the slashes they inflicted.

XIII

Cuando estaban peliando
Llegó el padre de uno
—Hijo mío de mi corazón
No pelees con ninguno.

XIV

—Quítese de aquí mi padre
Que ando más bravo que
un lion
No me haga usar mi espada
Y le traspase el corazón.

XV

—Hijo mío desobediente
Por lo que acabas de hablar
Antes que el sol se meta
La vida te han de quitar.

XVI

En fin el hijo desobediente
En una vez dio un tropezón
El otro con aguilez
Le punzó el corazón.

XVII

Él mal herido de rodillas
Suspirando cayó al suelo
Poniendo en fin la riña
De dos varones su duelo.

XVIII

Esto fue lo que le pasó
Al que a su padre amenazó
Como no obedecer a su padre
Hasta la vida perdió.

XIX

Al hijo desobediente
Se arrima su padre diciendo:
—Si tú me has obedecido
No te viera yo muriendo.

XIII

When they were fighting
One of their fathers arrived
"My dear, beloved son,
Don't fight with anyone."

XIV

"Get out of here my father
For I'm madder than hell
Don't make me use my sword
To traverse your own heart."

XV

"My dear disobedient son
Because of what you've just said
Before the sun has set
You shall lose your life."

XVI

Finally the disobedient son
All at once stumbled over
His enemy in his agile form
Had pierced his heart.

XVII

Badly wounded and on his knees
Sighing, he fell to the ground
Putting an end to the squabble
Their duel would be no more.

XVIII

This is what happened to him
To the one who threatened
his father
By not obeying his father
He ended up losing his life.

XIX

As for the disobedient son
His father said to him:
"If you had just obeyed me
I wouldn't be seeing you die."

XX

—*La culpa sólo fue mía*
Padre de mi corazón
Perdóneme padre mío
Y écheme su bendición.

XXI

—*Hijo mío yo te perdono*
Y te doy mi bendición
Y le pido a Dios Celestial
Que de Él alcances perdón.

XXII

Miren señores lo que pasa
Con el celo y la ira
Cuando dos varones
se encuentran
Queriéndose quitar la vida.

XXIII

Siete versitos de este corrido
El nombre del autor no lo sé
Con diez y seis versitos más
La tragedia yo completé.

XXIV

Yo completé este corrido
Para que supieran que pasó
Cuando dos hombres peliando
Uno al otro mató.

XXV

Mi nombre no se los doy
Porque nunca ha sido
compositor
Sólo Le[s] desea buena suerte
a todos
Este humilde servidor.

XX

"The fault was all mine
My dear beloved father
Forgive me, father of mine
And give me your blessing."

XXI

"My dear son I forgive you
And I give you my blessing
And I ask God Almighty
That He too forgive you."

XXII

Look at what happens,
my friends,
From jealousy and wrath
When two fellows confront
each other
Wanting to take each other's life.

XXIII

Seven little verses to this ballad
The name of the author I
know not
With sixteen more small verses
I've completed this tragedy.

XXIV

I've completed this ballad
So you'd know what happened
When two men got to fighting
One ended up killing the other.

XXV

I won't give you my name
Because I've never been a poet
I only wish everyone good luck
This very humble servant
of yours.

XXVI

Aquí el fin de este corrido
Del hijo desobediente
Un buen ejemplo para todos
Los que se crean muy
valientes.

XXVI

Here is the end of this ballad,
That concerns the disobedient
son.
It's a good example to all of those
Who think of themselves as
courageous.

Edumenio Lovato

Corrido de Juan Valdez

The Ballad of Juan Valdez

I

El mil nuevecientos ocho
Vayan poniendo cuidado
Mataron a Juan Valdez
El día cuatro de mayo.

I

In nineteen hundred and eight
Start paying attention now
They killed Juan Valdez
On the fourth day of May.

II

El día cuatro de mayo
De nadie se despidió
Su sangre en la pared
Que fue lo que les dejó.

II

On the fourth day of May
He said good-bye to no one
His blood [splattered] on the wall
Is all he left them.

III

El día cuatro de mayo
La desgracia ha sucedido
Mataron a Juan Valdez
Pero lo mataron dormido
¡A qué hombres tan
inhumanos
Y tan fuera de sentido!

III

On the fourth day of May
The day the tragedy occurred
They killed Juan Valdez
But they did so while he slept
Oh such wretched and cruel men
And so lacking in common sense!

IV

Pues uno de sus hijitos [9]
Que fue el que los vido entrar
A Alvino Gurulé y a
Emiliano Sandoval
Tambien a Antonio José
El que lo iba asesinar.

IV

One of his small children [9]
Who was the one to see
Alvino Gurulé and Emiliano
Sandoval enter
Also [saw] Antonio José
Who was going to assassinate
him [Juan Valdez].

V

El finado Juan Valdez
Tenía a su hijita en un lado
Pobrecita huerfanita
A padecer la han dejado
Era huérfana de madre
Bien lo sabe este condado
Le mataron a su padre
Que es lo que le había quedado.

VI

Luego que ya le mataron
Se pusieron a pensar
A hacerle su sepultura
Le llevaron a un corral
Y estaba la tierra dura
No le pudieron sepultar.

VII

Le llevaron arrastrando
Con muy grande inotomía
Y su sangre derramando
Porque sesos no tenía
Se quedaron en la casa
En la cama en que dormía.

VIII

Válgame Santa María
De Santuario de Jerez
Con muy grande inotomía
Mataron a Juan Valdez
Le bañaron en su sangre
De la cabeza a los pies.

IX

Condado de Sandoval
Ven da tu declaración
Un hecho tan criminal
Que pasó en El Cabezón
No se puede perdonar
Mucho menos sin razón.

V

The deceased Juan Valdez
Had his small daughter at his side
Poor, unfortunate little orphan
She has been left to suffer
She was already motherless
It is well known in this county
Now they've killed her father
The only thing she had left.

VI

Then after they murdered him
They began to think [about]
Whether to bury him or not
They took him to a corral
But the earth there was very hard
So they couldn't bury him.

VII

They dragged him [his body]
With such great cruelty
And with his blood gushing out,
Because he had no brains
They were left at home
In the bed where he slept.

VIII

"Please help me," Saint Mary,
From the Sanctuary at Jerez
For it was with such great cruelty
That they killed Juan Valdez
They soaked him in his own blood
From his head down to his toes.

IX

County of Sandoval
Come make your statement
Regarding such a criminal act
That happened in Cabezón
Which cannot be forgiven
Especially without an
explanation.

X

Precinto Número Tres
Quien explicarte pudiera
Mira lo que sucedió
Publicado en La Bandera*
La culpa no tuve yo
Que este asesinato sucediera.

XI

Quién tuviera tinta de oro
Y una pluma de acero
Para escribir esta cantada
Para que lo sepa el mundo
entero
En Arizona mentada
La compuso un borreguero.

XII

El que compuso esta cantada
No ha sido compositor
Su nombre es Juan Jaramillo
Lo siento de corazón
Dios se lo lleve a su Gloria
Y tenga de su alma perdón.

X

Precinct Number Three
If only someone could explain
Look at what has happened
[It is] published in *La Bandera**
The fault was not mine at all
That this murder occurred.

XI

If only someone had gold ink
And a pen made of steel
With which to write this song
Then the whole world
would know
That in celebrated Arizona
A sheepherder composed it.

XII

He who composed this song
Is not really a composer
His name is Juan Jaramillo
I regret it from my heart
May God take him to heaven
And have mercy on his soul.

*A Newspaper published in Albuquerque during the 1930s.

EDUMENIO LOVATO

Tragedia de Antonio Lerma*

The Tragedy of Antonio Lerma*

I

Año de mil nuevecientos
¡A qué año tan desgraciado!
Murió don Antonio Lerma
El día último de mayo.

I

It was in nineteen hundred
Oh what a terrible year!
Don Antonio Lerma died
On the last day of May.

*A well-known Sandoval County political figure.

II

El miércoles en la tarde
Cuando el huracán llegó
Lo mataron en su tienda
Y encerrado se quedó
Cristianos tengan inmienda
Miren lo que sucedió.

III

Entre las cuatro y las cinco
Le salieron a buscar
Le buscaron en la plaza
Y no le pudieron hallar
Le prepararon su mesa
Para que fuera a cenar.

IV

Ya fueron por don Lorenzo
Para que le viniera a buscar
Anduvo cuarto por cuarto
En fin no le pudo hallar.

V

En trataron de abrir
Pues el cuarto de la tienda
Señores con otra llave
Para que mejor me
entiendan.

VI

Luego que abrieron la puerta
Válgame el cielo adorado
Fue lo que vieron primero
A don Antonio tirado.

VII

El cuerpo era boca abajo
Tenía su sombrero a un lado
Y en la bolsa de su chaleco
Tenía su reló quebrado.

II

It was Wednesday afternoon
When the hurricane struck
He was killed in his store
Where he was left locked up
All you Christians have pity
Just look at what's happened.

III

Between four and five o'clock
They went to look for him
They looked for him at the plaza
But they couldn't find him
They prepared supper for him
So that he could eat.

IV

They've already gone for
Don Lorenzo
So that he could come look
for Lerma
Lorenzo went from room to room
But finally gave up on him.

V

They [the neighbors] tried and
tried to open
The room to his store
Try another key, my friends,
Maybe you'll have better luck.

VI

As soon as they opened the door
Heaven help us all
The first thing they saw
Was Don Antonio on the floor.

VII

He was lying face down
With his hat by his side
And in his vest pocket
Was his watch, now smashed.

VIII

Tenía una rodilla doblada
Para que mejor me entiendan
Los pies para el escritorio
Y la sangre hasta la puerta.

IX

Luego que ya le tendieron
Luego que ya le lavaron
De los pies a la cabeza
¿Estaba disfigurado?

X

Pobre doña Ana María
Con que dolor lloraba
Pobrecita la Angelita
A quién le dirá papá.

XI

Salieron las telégrafas
Y los correos mensuales
Ya les fueron las noticias
A todos los principales.

XII

Salen todos sus amigos [los
de Lerma]
Corriendo como asustados
Sólo de ver a su amigo
En la infamia que
le hallaron.

XIII

Los que mataron a Lerma
Sólo Dios sabrá
Mi madre tiene un perrito
Mi madre lo matará
Del cuerito hará un tambor
Lo que fuere sonará.

VIII

He had one knee bent
So you'll understand what
I'm saying
His feet were facing the desk
And his blood [flowed] to the door.

IX

As soon as they laid him down
As soon as they washed him
From his head to his toes
They saw he was all disfigured.

X

Poor Doña Ana María
How she cried and cried
Poor little Angelita
Whom will she call Dad?

XI

The telegraph news has gone out
And as for the monthly
announcements
The news has already been sent
to them
As well as to all of their suscribers.

XII

All of his [Antonio Lerma's]
friends come out
Running as if scared
Just from seeing their friend
Found in such infamy.

XIII

Those who murdered Lerma
God only knows
My mother has a puppy
My mother shall kill him
From the hide she'll make a drum
Whatever sounds come out,
come out.

XIV
¡Hora lo verán Corrales!
¡Hora lo verá Alameda!
¡Hora lo verán señores!
Si les hace falta Lerma.

XV
Dicen que en su huerta de uva
Señores se sepultó
No más siete pies de tierra
De su caudal ocupó.

XVI
Aquí se acaba esta tragedia
Válgame el cielo adorado
Se cortó una buena rienda
Que estaba en este condado.

XIV
Now you'll see, Corrales!
Now you'll see, Alameda!
Now you'll see, my friends!
Whether you'll miss Lerma or not.

XV
They say that in his vineyard
He was buried ladies and
gentlemen
All he took from his fortune
Was seven feet of soil.

XVI
This tragedy ends here
May God have mercy on me
We've lost a good citizen
Who lived in this county.

EDUMENIO LOVATO

*Corrido de un vaquero**

I
En el Condado de Sandoval
entero
Todos tristes sentirán
La muerte de un caballero
Por patas de un caballo
alazán.

II
Adiós los Ojos Calientes
En donde fui nacido y criado
*Adiós plaza de La Posta***
Del Río Puerco afamado
Donde Dios me envió la muerte
En las patas de un caballo.

The Ballad of a Cowboy

I
Throughout Sandoval County
Everyone will feel lonely
Because of the death of a
cowboy
By the hoofs of a sorrel horse.

II
Good-bye to Hot Springs
Where I was born and raised
Good-bye village of La Posta**
On the renowned Río Puerco
Where God commanded my death
By the hoofs of a horse.

* New Mexico–type ballad.
** Today known as El Cabezón.

III

Madres las que tengan hijitos
Mi corazón triste grita
Les encargo a mis amigos
Duélasen de mi hijita
Que en este mundo se queda
Esta infeliz huerfanita.

IV

Me trajeron al doctor
A nada pudo acudir
Y sólo vino a avisar
A que horas iba a morir.

V

Día viernes a las tres
Cuando me tocó espirar
Y el sábado me llevaron
A donde me iban a enterrar.

VI

Se nos acabó Rafael
Le dice doña Altagracia
Suelta el llanteo doña Emilia
Y les dice, ¡qué desgracia!
Madrecita de mi vida
¡Ay qué obscura queda
mi casa!

VII

Caballo estima mentado
Que tú la muerte me dites
Mi cuerpo está sepultado
Y de sangre le tiñiste.

VIII

Adiós todos mis amigos
Pido a todos el favor
Que no tengan engremiento
Que esta vida es un vapor
En cualquier momento
Ya no se ve ni rumor.

III

Mothers who have children
My sad heart cries out
I beg of my friends
To take pity on my daughter
Who is left in this world
An unhappy little orphan.

IV

They brought me to the doctor
But he couldn't do anything
And he came only to tell me
What time I was going to die.

V

It was Friday at 3 o'clock
When my time to expire arrived
And on Saturday they took me
Where they were going to bury me.

VI

Rafael is no longer with us
Says Doña Altagracia [to her]
Doña Emilia bursts out crying
And says, what a misfortune!
Holy dear Mother of God
My house is so gloomy!

VII

Horse you shall be mentioned
For you're the one who killed me
My body has been buried
Along with the blood that
stained [the body].

VIII

Farewell to all of my friends
I ask of you one favor
And let it not be in vain
Know that this life is like vapor
And at any given moment
Not even a murmur is heard.

EDUARDO VALDEZ

Corrido de un vaquero

I

Yo vivo en los campos
Mi casa es muy fea
El techo se ocupa
Por la chiminea.

II

Si algún día fueres
Al Rincón de Marcos
Verás qué difícil
Verás qué trabajo.

III

Verás una choza
No es alta es baja
Y quien la compuso
Jesús y Apodaca.

IV

Mi casa es de rama
No tiene sotella
El techo se ocupa
Por la chimineya.

V

Y ventanas tiene
Como el cielo estreyas
Que cuando no llueve
Pues no se goteya.

VI

Ésta es la vida
Que pasa un vaquero
Que para amasar
Usa su sombrero.

The Ballad of a Cowboy

I

I live in the countryside
My house is very ugly
The roof holds up
The chimney.

II

If someday you should go
To Rincón de Marcos
You'll see how difficult
You'll see how hard life is.

III

You'll see a shanty
It isn't tall but short
And he who built it
Is Jesús Apodaca.

IV

My house is made of branches
It doesn't have a flat roof
The roof holds up
The chimney.

V

The windows that it has
Are like the star-filled sky
When it doesn't rain
It [the house] doesn't leak.

VI

This is the life
That a cowboy lives
For mixing dough
He uses his hat.

VII

Y de charola usa
Una garra de cuero
Cuece sus galletas
Entre el cenicero.

VIII

Que a gusto me siento
Cuando echo tortillas
Unas salen crudas
Otras bien cocidas.

IX

Unas redonditas
Otras con esquinas
También salen pintas
Otras mascarillas.

X

En un rincón tengo
Mis espuelas colgadas
Pues van los ratones
Las usan de guitarra.

XI

Quizás hacen baile
Seguro con ellas
Porque en la harina
Yo encuentro la huella.

XII

Debajo mi almuada
Oigo estar tocando
Las vívoras pasan
Cuasi galopiando.

XIII

Todos mis vecinos
Que son los coyotes
Que bonitas polcas
Tocan en las noches.

VII

And for a pan he uses
A piece of hide
He cooks his biscuits
In the middle of the ash pit.

VIII

How good I feel
When I make tortillas
Some come out half-baked
Others are overcooked.

IX

Some are really round
Others have corners
They also come out spotted
Others are half masked (burned)

X

In a corner
My spurs are hanging
Then along come mice and
Use them for guitars.

XI

Perhaps they dance
To a tune they play on them
Because in the flour
I find their tracks.

XII

Underneath my pillow
I hear music playing
Then snakes go by
Almost galloping.

XIII

All of my neighbors
Who are the coyotes
What beautiful polkas
They play at night.

XIV

Ellos tocan polcas
Quadrillas y chotes
Los pobres zorrillos
Vacilan al trote.

XV

Si gallinas hubiera
Peor la ruina fuera
Porque ellas se bañan
En el cenicero.

XIV

They play polkas
Quartets and schottisches
The poor skunks
Flirt in a trot.

XV

If there were chickens
Matters would be worse
Because they bathe
In the ash pit.

NOTES

1. Quelite, a ballad of Mexican origin, is also the name of a town in the state of Sinaloa in west-central Mexico.

2. San Ignacio is a Mexican village near Quelite.

3. Puebla, one of Mexico's major cities, lies southeast of Mexico City.

4. *Carretera* is not a common term in rural New Mexico; therefore, it seems somewhat misplaced in this New Mexican ballad.

5. Nuestra Señora de Guadalupe, the patron saint of Guadalupe, Spain, is also the patron saint of Mexico. She has a huge following in New Mexico.

6. The word *pantalla*, or movie screen, like *carretera* above in Note 4, is not a common word in New Mexico Spanish.

7. *Fonógrafo* is in reference to the Victrola phonograph player popular in the 1920s.

8. According to Rubén Cobos, this ballad may have originated in Spain as a *romance vulgar*, a type of ballad composed and recited by a street-corner poet. Cobos informed me that the version presented here has the original stanzas plus Mexican and New Mexican stanzas added to it.

9. Juan Valdez was a widower with three children when he was murdered. His children were Soraida, Jacobo, and Avelino, who was mentally retarded. A story about Avelino by Benny Lucero appears in Chapter 3.

ANTONIO PADILLA GARCÍA, ABOUT TWENTY YEARS OLD, IN GUADALUPE, N.M., C. 1927.
PHOTO COURTESY OF THE AUTHOR.

CHAPTER 5

CHIQUIAOS

POETIC QUATRAINS

UNLIKE DICHOS, ADIVINANZAS, OR CORRIDOS, WHICH HAVE THEIR ROOTS in Spain, the *chiquiao*, or poetic quatrain, seems to have been invented by people in Northern New Mexico. To the best of my knowledge, no comprehensive study on the chiquiao exists, so it is difficult to pinpoint the time, place, and circumstance of its first appearance. What we do know is that the chiquiao was recited in a flirtatious manner, and it was used primarily at dances. It was a means by which one engaged in dialogue with members of the opposite sex. A man customarily assumed the initiative role, and the woman played along by responding positively or negatively to the male's overtures. As described by Cleofas M. Jaramillo, the chiquiao was a unique dance game, ostensibly formal and somewhat controlled; it engaged only a select few and perhaps even rich people more than common folks. As she says:

> *El Chiquiado* [*sic*] waltz was danced by a few who had the gift of verse. The dancers waltzed around the hall until the leading couple came opposite the chair placed in the middle of the floor. The man placed his lady partner on the chair, sang or recited a verse to her and walked to the crowd of men standing by the door. He chose two men and brought them back, one on each arm, and presented them to his lady. If the verse each one recited to her did not please her she disdainfully turned her face away. Her partner went back to another two, until he found one whose verse pleased her. She then arose and finished the waltz with him.[1]

A slightly different perspective on the chiquiao is provided by Charles Aranda in his booklet *Dichos: Proverbs and Sayings from the Spanish*. *"Chiquillados"* [*sic*], he writes, "were short verses recited by a man either to humor or to impress a woman he wanted to dance with. If the woman accepted the verse, she would get up and dance."[2] An even more succinct explanation of this folkloric jewel is written by Rubén Cobos, who says that a chiquiao is "a dance game during which poetic quatrains are exchanged by the participants."[3]

Over the years I have interviewed many older people in both Northern New Mexico and in southern Colorado on a number of topics related to folklore. Those with any knowledge about chiquiaos described them in a rather rudimentary way without much detail or fanfare. Even my maternal grandmother characterized them merely as "fun" kinds of things to "kill time" with, as it were. She concurred with others that chiquiaos were poetic compositions exchanged primarily by adult men and women at dances held in local villages. On occasion young folks exchanged chiquiaos as well.[4] Among the young, poetic quatrains were looked upon as romantic notions that often led to courtship and marriage.

The word *chiquiao* derives from *chiquear* (*chiquiar*), which means to pamper or to spoil someone. Used in the reflexive (*chiquearSE*), the connotation changes a bit; it indicates one wants to be begged or coaxed. *"Ella se chiquea con él"* means "She wants to be coaxed by him."

One social custom young and old men and women practiced in the Río Puerco Valley was the recitation of chiquiaos. These humorous or flattering poems were at times risqué and insulting. As a young boy, I can recall grown-ups giggling between musical numbers, perhaps exchanging a chiquiao or two, while the *bastonero* (floor manager) collected from the men money to pay the musicians. Verses were offered by a married man to a married woman (not his wife) or to a young lady. They also were presented by a young man to a young woman. In either case, chiquiaos were recited for fun.

In terms of its spirit and the punch it carries, the chiquiao is reminiscent of the Spanish *piropo*, a form of flattery used among boys and girls. Until recently, it enjoyed popularity throughout Spain. This was certainly true in the 1960s when I attended the University of Granada in Andalucía. There I heard piropos all the time among university students. Today the piropo is heard infrequently on college campuses and seldom in the streets of large metropolises such as Madrid, perhaps because many young people consider the piropo old-fashioned. Just the opposite is true, for example, of small rural Spanish communities in Andalucía and Extremadura. In these provinces, the piropo is still heard among the young.

Most of the chiquiaos in this chapter deal with love and its attendant states, including joy, passion, affection, tenderness, despondency, sadness, despair, pain, and longing. We may consider the chiquiaos exceedingly romantic and altogether unrealistic in their description, scope, and tone. Nevertheless, people had fun with them; indeed, they are an example of the creative genius that sprang forth in moments of fun and levity. These four-line stanzas usually have octosyllabic verses. Unlike the dichos and adivinanzas, chiquiaos tend to adhere to a rhyme scheme, at times inconsistently maintaining octosyllabic verses, and sometimes violating the four-line stanza. The poetic quatrains are listed alphabetically by author, and for each piece, I have identified a specific theme knowing full well that the broader subject of each chiquiao is love. Some of the following chiquiaos were taught to me by my grandmother when I was a young boy. With my friends, I used the last three chiquiaos in my repertoire to flirt with girls during recess in the schoolyard.

CHIQUIAOS/POETIC QUATRAINS

NASARIO GARCÍA

De la pera no comí,
del vino bebí una gota.
Del besito que te di,
dulce me quedó la boca.

TEMA: Afección

From the pear I did not eat,
from the wine I took a few sips.
From the small kiss I gave you,
my mouth turned sweet like your lips.

THEME: Affection

Que bonito vas creciendo,
del tamaño d'esta casa.
Ya me estoy apreviniendo,
para dar las calabazas.

TEMA: Rechazo

My but you're growing up,
as big as this house.
I'm getting myself pumped up,
to toss you out like a mouse.

THEME: Rejection

Pasé por Las Lagunitas, y me jui por Cochití. Pa estar en la resolana, lo mismo es allá que aquí. *TEMA: Indiferencia*	I went by Las Lagunitas, and I passed thru Cochití. Whether I'm in the sun or not, being here or there matters not. THEME: Indifference
Ai viene saliendo el sol, rodeao de campanitas. Dichoso de los solteros, que gozan de las bonitas. *TEMA: Envidia*	There's the sun coming out, surrounded by little bells. Lucky are the bachelors, who can enjoy the pretty girls. THEME: Jealousy
En una mesa te puse, un plato con elotes. No lo hago por que me quieras, si no por que te alborotes. *TEMA: Coquetear*	I place on a table for you, a plate full of ears of sweet corn. I don't do it so you'll like me, but rather so you'll find me enticing. THEME: Flirting
Cuando naranjas, naranjas, cuando limones, limones, cuando tú te peinas, que bonita te pones. *TEMA: Adulación*	When it's oranges, it's oranges, when it's lemons, it's lemons. Whenever you comb your hair, you cause everyone to stare. THEME: Flattery
Cuando naranjas, naranjas, cuando limones, limones, cuando tú caminas, que bonita te pones. *TEMA: Adulación*	When it's oranges, it's oranges, when it's lemons, it's lemons. Whenever you take a walk, you cause everyone to stare. THEME: Flattery

EDUMENIO LOVATO

Te pido humildemente
un favor,
que no me eches en olvido
Que algún día nos veremos,
si nuestro Dios es servido.

    TEMA: *Esperanza*

I humbly ask you a favor,
please don't forget me.
For one day we'll meet again,
if the good Lord is willing.

    THEME: Hope

A los ángeles del cielo,
les he de mandar a pedir,
una pluma de sus alas,
para poderte escribir,
uno o dos renglones,
que no te puedo claramente
decir.

    TEMA: *Pasión*

The angels in the heavens,
of them I shall request,
a feather from their wings,
so that I can scribble to you,
one or two written lines,
that I cannot at the moment
express clearly.

    THEME: Passion

Desde el día que tú te fuistes,
en mi corazón siento un dolor.
Ni los pajaritos cantan,
ni los árboles dan flor.

    TEMA: *Melancolía*

Since the day you left,
I've felt an ache in my heart.
Even the birds quit singing,
and the trees ceased budding.

    THEME: Dejection

Soñaba profundamente,
y tu rostro contemplaba.
Y en mi sueño lentamente,
vida y expresión te daba.

    TEMA: *Afecto profundo*

I was dreaming profoundly,
contemplating your face.
And slowly in my dreams,
your face took on form and life.

    THEME: Deep affection

Asomaste tus labios rojos,
y encantadora sonrisa.
Y de tus bonitos ojos,
llanto corría precisa.

    TEMA: *Tristeza*

You showed your red lips,
and your charming smile.
And from your beautiful eyes,
tears flowed down your cheeks.

    THEME: Sadness

Este páramo disierto,
es la imagen de mi vida.
El árbol de hojas cubierto,
eres tú prenda querida.

TEMA: Desaliento

This bleak desert,
is the image of my life.
The leaf-covered tree
is you, object of my affection.

THEME: Despondency

De los chinos de tu frente,
me darás una semilla,
para sembrar en el Oriente,
una rosa de castilla,
para tenerte presente,
a todas horas del día.

TEMA: Anhelo

From your forehead's curls,
you shall give me a seed.
For me to sow in the East,
a pretty red rose,
So I may have you present,
at all hours of the day.

THEME: Longing

Tengo un nicho de cristal,
hecho de tus finas manos.
Para colocarte en él,
si siguemos como vamos.
Pero si me pagas mal,
de seguro lo quebramos.

TEMA: Inquietud

I have a niche made of crystal,
made by your fine hands.
To place you in it,
if we continue on this road.
But should you deceive me,
we will certainly break it [the niche].

THEME: Trepidation

Sobre una mesa te vide,
dibujando en un papel.
Parecías una rosa,
en un nicho de oropel.

TEMA: La belleza

I saw you leaning over a table,
drawing on a piece of paper.
You looked like a rose,
reflected in an aluminum niche.

THEME: Beauty

Blanca flor de la lemita,
morada de garambullo.
Vente trigueña conmigo,
que este corazón es tuyo.

TEMA: Ternura

White flower of the squawbush,
dressed in gooseberry.
Come along with me darling,
since this heart is all yours.

THEME: Tenderness

Me prestarás tu pañuelo,
para limpiarme el sudor.
Para ver si se me pega,
la nobleza de tu amor.
TEMA: Fuerte cariño

Lend me your kerchief,
to wipe off my sweat.
To see if the nobility,
of your love attaches itself to me.
THEME: Strong attachment

Tengo un ramo de verjeles,
traspuesto y en un decoro.
Te he de pesar en dos fieles,
y una balanza de oro.
Para saber si me quieres,
lo tanto que yo te adoro.
TEMA: Incertidumbre

I have a bouquet of
garden flowers,
which I picked and
arranged decoratively.
I shall weigh you on two
pointers of balance,
on a scale made of gold.
To find out if you love me,
as much as I adore you.
THEME: Uncertainty

Pajarito amarillito,
colorsito de limón.
¿Cómo quieres que te cante,
si me duele el corazón?
TEMA: Sensibilidad

Little yellow bird,
the color of a lemon.
How can I sing to you,
if my heart aches?
THEME: Sensitivity

Eres uno y eres dos,
eres tres y eres cuarenta.
Y eres puerta de dos manos,
donde mi corazón entra.
TEMA: Devoción

You are one and you are two,
you are three and you are forty.
And you are a door with
two handles,
through which my heart enters.
THEME: Devotion

Arbolito enflorecido,
donde mi corazón se divierte.
Entre más estoy contigo,
más ganas me dan de verte.
TEMA: Alegría

Little tree in full bloom,
where my heart enjoys itself.
The longer I am with you,
the more I yearn to see you.
THEME: Happiness

De tu ventana a la mía,
me tirastes un limón.
El limón me dio en el pecho,
y el zumo en el corazón.

TEMA: *Travesuras*

From your window to mine,
you tossed me a lemon.
The lemon hit my chest,
and its juice my heart.

THEME: Playfulness

Tu hermosura me provoca,
de verte tan delgadita.
Volqué tu nariz, tu boca,
no te feriaría por otra,
anque sella más bonita.

TEMA: *Devoción*

Your beauty concerns me,
when I see you so thin.
I tilted your nose, your mouth,
still, I won't exchange you for
someone else,
even though she may be more
beautiful.

THEME: Devotion

Ya no me entretiene el oro,
ni me entretiene el metal.
Sólo por tu ausencia lloro,
en este triste lugar.

TEMA: *Abatimiento*

Gold no longer entertains me,
metal doesn't entertain me either.
Only because you're not here,
I cry in this lonely place.

THEME: Despair

No estrañas al verte triste,
te encuentre niña más bella.
Que siempre a cesar la noche,
tienen más luz las estrellas.

TEMA: *Esperanza*

I am not estranged by your
sad look,
the sadder you look, the more
beautiful you are.
Always at the end of each night,
the stars in the sky appear
brighter to me.

THEME: Hope

¿Sabes a quién te pareces,
ahora que te estoy mirando?
A la luna cuando sale,
y al sol cuando está brillando,
y la más fresca amapola,
cuando viene reventando.

TEMA: *Coqueteo*

Do you know whom you resemble,
now that I'm looking at you?
The moon when it comes out,
and the sun when it's shining.
As well as the freshest poppy,
when it slowly starts bursting out.

THEME: Flirting/teasing

Dicen que me han de matar,
por un amor verdadero.
Y en mi pecho han de quedar,
siete puñales de acero.
Yo en agonía he de estar,
y he de decir que te quiero.

TEMA: *Afecto profundo*

They say that I must die,
because of an amorous
relationship.
And my chest must suffer,
seven stabs from a steel knife.
I shall suffer moments of agony
for I must say that I love you.

THEME: Deep affection

Dicen que me han de quitar,
que te traiga en la memoria.
Primero se han de voltiar,
como los cubos de noria.
Y me he de sentar en tus brazos,
como San Pedro en la gloria.

TEMA: *Afecto sincero*

They say I must get rid of you,
who I bear in my memory.
First they must turn
me upside down,
like a bucket in an artesian well.
Then I will end up in your arms,
just as sure as St. Peter is
in Heaven.

THEME: Sincere affection

Tengo un cepillito de oro,
y un peinecito de plata.
Para peinarte esos chinos,
que esos son los que me matan.

TEMA: *Desconsuelo*

I have a little gold brush,
and a little silver comb.
So that I can comb those curls,
for they are what's killing me.

THEME: Despair

Sobre una mesa te puse,
bolitas de oro en un plato.
Cada vez que sale el sol,
me acuerdo de tu retrato.
Miro lo que es el amor,
jovencito no seas ingrato.

TEMA: *Ingratitud*

I placed on the table for you,
a plateful of tiny gold nuggets.
Every time the sun comes out,
I remember your face.
I see what to me is true love,
my dear young man don't
be ungrateful.

THEME: Ungratefulness

Quisiera ser pajarito,
para volar y irte a ver,
para no estarte escribiendo,
y hacer al mundo saber,
de lo que nos hemos querido,
y nos hemos de querer.
TEMA: *Enamoramiento*

I would like to be a little bird,
so I could fly to see you,
so I wouldn't have to be writing,
and letting the whole
world know,
how much we have loved
each other,
and we shall continue to do so.
THEME: Infatuation

Si fuera papel volara,
si fuera tinta tiñera.
Si fuera estampa pegara,
y contigo mismo hablara.
TEMA: *Anhelo*

If I were paper I would fly,
if I were ink I would tinge.
If I were a postage stamp, I'd
stick [to the envelope],
and with you I would converse.
THEME: Desire

Tengo una sala medida,
con cien yardas de listón.
En cada esquina una rosa,
y en medio tu corazón.
TEMA: *Alegría*

I have a hall already measured,
with one hundred yards of ribbon.
In every corner is a rose,
and right in the center is
your heart.
THEME: Happiness

Tus ojos son un lucero,
tus ojos son un nivel.
No hay otros ojos tan echiceros,
como los tuyos cuando me ven.
TEMA: *Travesuras*

Your eyes are like a bright star,
your eyes are like a spirit's level.
No other eyes are so charming,
as yours when you look at me.
THEME: Mischief

Eres chiquito y bonito,
así como eres te quiero.
Pareces ser echisito,
manos de un platero.
Tu boquita de coral,
y tus labios de caramelo.
TEMA: *Ternura*

You're tiny and cute,
that's just the way I like you.
You seem to be exquisite,
like the hands of a silversmith.
Your mouth resembling coral,
and your lips those of sugar candy.
THEME: Tenderness

Que bonita vas creciendo,
como una espiga de trigo.
Ya me estoy apreviniendo,
para casarme contigo.

TEMA: Fuerte afecto

My but you're turning pretty,
like a tassel of wheat.
I'm getting myself ready,
to marry you.

THEME: Affection

Entre jardines me acuesto,
y en flores tiendo mi cama.
Rosita no te corté,
porque no me dio la gana.
No porque no me acordé,
lucero de la mañana.

TEMA: Despego

I go to bed in gardens,
and the flowers are my bed.
I did not cut a small rose,
because I didn't feel like it.
Not because I didn't remember,
my bright morning star.

THEME: Indifference

El ser negro no es afrente,
no es color que quita fama.
Si el zapato negro luce,
en la más pulida dama.

TEMA: Vislumbre

Being black is not an affront,
it's not a color that
diminishes fame.
Why a black shoe can shine,
on the most beautiful lady.

THEME: Appearance

De la pera no comí,
del vino bebí una gota.
Del besito que te di,
dulce me quedó la boca.

TEMA: Ternura

From the pear I did not eat,
of the wine I took a few sips.
From the small kiss I gave you,
my mouth turned sweet like
your lips.

THEME: Tenderness

Eres lindo sin tamaño,
lindo sin comparación.
Lindos tu padre y tu madre,
y toda tu generación.

TEMA: Adulación

You're handsome without match,
handsome without comparison.
Beautiful are your father
and mother,
and this includes all of
your relations.

THEME: Flattery

Por la luna doy un peso,
por el sol doy un tostón.
Por los chinos de tu frente,
la vida y el corazón.

TEMA: *Compromiso*

For the moon I'll give a dollar,
for the sun I'll give fifty cents.
For the curls on your forehead,
I'll give you my heart and soul.

THEME: Commitment

Eres clavel, eres rosa,
eres clavo de comer.
Eres el más lindo mozo,
que en el mundo pueda haber.

TEMA: *Coqueteo*

You're a carnation, a rose,
you're an edible.
You're the most handsome chap,
that's ever walked on this earth.

THEME: Flirting

En lo alto de sol escribo,
la forma de tu carrera.
Si quieres que yo te olvide,
pídele a Dios que me muera.
Porque viva es imposible olvidar,
a quien yo quiera.

TEMA: *Fuerte apego*

I sketch at the heat of the day,
the shape of your running
physique.
If you want me to forget you,
ask God to make me die.
Because while alive I can't forget,
the person whom I love.

THEME: Fondness

La águila para volar,
busca la tierra caliente.
Y el hombre para nombrar,
busca muchacha decente.
Para poderse parar,
donde se para la gente.

TEMA: *Dignidad*

For the eagle to fly,
it looks for warm soil.
And for a man to excel,
he looks for a decent girl.
In order to stand tall,
wherever people congregate.

THEME: Dignity

Toma esta cajita de oro,
mira lo que viene adentro.
Tiene celos, tiene amores,
tiene muchos sentimientos.

TEMA: *Emociones*

Take this small gold box,
look at what's inside.
It contains jealousy and love,
as well as many sentiments.

THEME: Emotions

ANÓNIMO/NAME OF DONOR WITHHELD UPON REQUEST

Pareces una rosa,	You look like a rose,
dentro de un jardín.	inside a garden.
Pareces una mierda,	You look like shit,
dentro de un bacín.	inside a bedpan.
TEMA: Desprecio	THEME: Rebuff

NOTES

1. Cleofas M. Jaramillo, *Shadows of the Past* (Santa Fe: Ancient City Press, 1972), 52.

2. Charles Aranda, *Dichos: Proverbs and Sayings from the Spanish* (Santa Fe: Sunstone Press, 1975), 56.

3. Rubén Cobos, *A Dictionary of New Mexico and Southern Colorado Spanish* (Santa Fe: Museum of New Mexico Press, 1983), 47. Cobos offers a more detailed study of the chiquiao in "The New Mexican Game of 'Valse chiquiao,'" *Western Folklore* 15 (1956): 95–101.

4. N. Howard (Jack) Thorp, an employee for the Workers' Progress Administration, in an entry entitled "Chiquiau—A Spanish Dance," provides a different slant on the *chiquiao* with young people, not older folks, playing a major role. Thorp puts it in this way: "One of the quaintest of the old Spanish dances, the chiquiau [*sic*], is performed in the following manner: When the music for the dance starts several boys approach the young lady whom they desire for their partner. The young lady is seated in a chair. The first boy to arrive recites a little verse to her and, when he is finished, she turns her head sideways showing him her profile. Then the next boy recites his poem and, again, upon the completion of the verse, the girl turns her head from him. This process continues until the last would-be partner has been heard. Then the girl arises and takes the arm of the boy whose verses has pleased her most. He is her partner for the dance. . . . This process causes the people sitting near the girl a great deal of amusement as all listen to the witty and sometimes extravagantly complimentary verses. When a particularly pretty girl is the subject, sometimes as many as a dozen young men rush over prepared to recite their most extravigant [*sic*] verses for her favors." Museum of New Mexico History Library (File 5, D. 5, Fo. 1).

RESIDENTS OF SAN LUIS, N.M., CELEBRATING FIRST HOLY COMMUNION, C. 1929–30.
COURTESY OF SALOMÓN LOVATO.

CHAPTER 6

CARTAS

LETTERS

COMMUNITIES SUCH AS CABEZÓN, GUADALUPE, CASA SALAZAR, AND SAN Luis had a semiofficial scribe, or *escribano*, who composed and answered letters for those who could not read or write. As far as I can ascertain, the scribe became literate of his own volition and perhaps had more formal education than most of his neighbors. Most so-called scribes seemed to have been men; however, there were women scribes as well. As a child in Guadalupe, I recall people saying, *"Voy a ver a doña Adelita a que me escriba una carta,"* or "I'm going to see Doña Adelita about writing a letter for me," and *"Tengo que hablar con Gabrielita pa que me componga una carta,"* or "I have to talk to Gabrielita so she can compose a letter for me." These two women, coincidentally, were the last two postmistresses—the latter in the 1940s and the former in the 1950s—before the community's demise in the late 1950s. They were relied upon for writing letters even though neither was considered an escribana because by that time most of the letter-writing customs discussed in this chapter had vanished.

The scribe was a very important person in the community. Sometimes his influence extended beyond village boundaries, especially if there was no scribe in the neighboring village. Like the priest, the scribe was a person people could trust with confidential information that could affect entire families. A tacit understanding regarding confidentiality between all parties existed as a code of honor. Whether it was a love letter or friendly correspondence was inconsequential; the scribe was bound to secrecy within and away from the village. It was an honorable position, and the scribe accepted his role with utmost dignity and little fanfare. Whether the scribe was compensated for services rendered or not is unclear, but charging a fee seems to have been the exception rather than the rule. Token gifts, including jerky and garden vegetables, were proffered.

The scribe's tasks were not limited to routine letter writing; rather, there were special cases and circumstances that required a more formal system of communication, such as letters related to baptisms and weddings. The language in these letters is more poetic than that of common correspondence, and it is marked by inconsistent orthography, but the format and structure and themes by which the addressees were addressed are much more formal. Different kinds of letters required special language, and while the written words may have been the scribe's, the thoughts he articulated were the sender's. The following letters, all prepared for different purposes, attest in great measure to the foregoing characteristics.

CARTA DE BAUTISMO — BAPTISMAL LETTER

Baptismal godparents, or *padrinos de bautismo*, were called upon to carry out the sacramental rites of the church after a child was born to a couple. A child's parents made a serious effort to have the baby baptized as soon after birth as possible, usually within thirty to forty days. The principal reason was the fact that a baby could fall ill and thus die without being anointed with the holy waters of baptism. In small communities of the Río Puerco Valley, baptizing a baby soon after birth was not easily accomplished since the priest visited the valley's villages only once a month. It was conceivable for the padrinos to travel to Jémez Springs or Cuba, which is where a priest resided, but a trip of that magnitude was difficult and rarely undertaken with a newborn baby.

The baby's parents, at times with the assistance of their own parents, made preparations for the baptism. This involved a number of simple events that engaged the immediate family; this was especially true if the child was the couple's first offspring. First came the parents' selection of the child's godparents, or *padrinos*. This was not a complicated process, yet it was at once informal and formal. If the child was the couple's firstborn, the mother's parents were asked to serve as godparents. The father's parents were next in line. Within the immediate or extended family, the procedure for asking was somewhat informal, and the request usually occurred during a special lunch on a Sunday afternoon or in the evening over coffee and dessert.

When prospective godparents were not part of the immediate or extended family, the process became more formal and complicated because friends and acquaintances were involved. Part of the formal procedure, particularly when would-be godparents were residents of another village, was to send a *carta de bautismo*, or baptismal letter, informing the addressees of the baby's arrival and inviting them to be the baby's godparents.

Higinio Griego and Mary Elsie García, Guadalupe, N.M., c. 1945. Photo courtesy of the author.

Such letters to the padrinos, as we shall see, were both formal and serious in tone. They expressed respect for the prospective godparents, who would as padrinos become engaged in an unbreakable bond with the godchild and the child's parents. Were anything tragic to happened to the child's parents, the godparents assumed responsibility for the godchild's physical, moral, and spiritual upbringing. Being a godparent was a joy and an honor, as well as an awesome undertaking, yet rarely did a couple decline such an invitation.

These letters were donated to me by Edumenio Lovato. They are formal in structure and serious in tone, and their language is a mixture of both formal and local lexicon. Note the use of both the local dialect with its orthographic tendencies commonly used by escribanos and the so-called standard Spanish (*derigir* for *dirigir*, *agan* for *hagan*, *llege for llegue*). These spelling characteristics are common today among Hispanic students from rural areas of New Mexico.

It is also interesting to examine the closing statement of the parties sending the letter. In the first letter they refer to themselves as "humble servants"; in the second letter the couple signs as "Your compadres," in anticipation of a positive answer or perhaps affirming a previously made agreement. Neither letter requests a response, but it was a foregone conclusion that the prospective compadres would indeed accept the invitation to become padrinos of the newborn child.

CARTA DE BAUTISMO

Bernalillo, Nuevo Méjico
Noviembre 3 de 1947

Señor Benceslado Gabaldón
y Marillita J. de Gabaldón

Apreciables Señores:

 Tomándonos la facultad y permiso de Uds., para derigir esta mal notada carta que llege a su presencia para saludar a ustedes y [el] resto de su casa. Pues les deseamos una buena y cabal salud. Pues nosotros todos buenos, gracias a Dios. Y siempre esperando que se agan sabedores del contenido de esta carta.

 Siendo que mi querida esposa dio a luz al mundo un niño el 29 de Octubre y como obligación y costumbre de nuestra religión hemos escojido, yo y mi esposa, a ustedes para que testifiquen el primer Sacramento sagrado a un niño que vino por primera ves al mundo, y rogando a Dios que atuen como padrinos, según los ritos de nuestra santa religión, partisipando desde hoy su amistad y respecto para lo futoro de nuestra vida.

 Quedando nosotros a su disposición de ustedes como humildes servidores,

  Frank L. Mora
  Filia A. Mora

BAPTISMAL LETTER

Bernalillo, New Mexico
November 3, 1947

Mister Benceslado Gabaldón
and Marillita J. de Gabaldón

My Dear Friends:

We allow ourselves the ability and your permission, hoping that this badly composed letter will get to you and greet you and the rest of your family as well. We wish you good and complete health. As for us, we are all well, thanks be to God. At the same time, we want you to take notice of the contents of this letter.

Since my dear wife gave birth to a child on the 29 of October, and according to tradition and custom of our religion, my wife and I have chosen you to witness the First Holy Sacrament of a child who came into this world for the first time, and praying to God that you will act as godparents, according to the rites of our holy religion, sharing from this day on in your friendship and respect of the future of our lives.

We remain at your disposal as your humble servants.

Frank L. Mora
Filia A. Mora

CARTA DE BAUTISMO

Domínguez, Nuevo Méjico
(San Luis, Nuevo Méjico)
Febrero 10, 1935

Señor Bencés Gabaldón
Señora Marillita Jaramillo de Gabaldón

Muy apreciables compadres,

Con el más alto respecto y cariño a saludarlos y después de saludarlos nos presentamos muy respetosamente ante el honor de Uds. a notificarles que el niño nacío el dia 21 de deciembre a las 8 de la tarde y nosotros con toda nuestra voluntad, los hemos escojido a ustedes para que sellan sus padrinos y lo lleven a la pila bautismal para que por medio de las aguas de Santo Bautismo nos ayuden aser de él un buen cristiano bajo de la iglesia Católica, Apostólica, Romana.

Con lo que nos despidemos deseándoles a ustedes mil veces felicidades.

Sus compadres,

Aparcio Lobato
Maclovia J. Lobato

BAPTISMAL LETTER

Domínguez, New Mexico
(San Luis, New Mexico)
February 10, 1935

Mr. Bencés Gabaldón
Mrs. Marillita Jaramillo de Gabaldón

My Dear Esteemed Compadres,

    With the utmost respect and affection, we would like to greet you and after doing so we would like respectfully before your honor to notify you of the child who was born on the 21st of December at 8:00 P.M. With all of our willingness we have chosen you to be his godparents [baptismal], and ask that you take him to the baptismal font so that by virtue of the holy water of the Holy Baptism you can help us make him a good Christian under the auspices of the Holy Catholic (Apostolic and Roman) Church.

    With this we bid you farewell wishing you happiness a thousand times over.

    Your compadres,

    Aparcio Lobato
    Maclovia J. Lobato

CARTA DE PEDIMENTO —
HAND-IN-MARRIAGE LETTER

When a boy wanted to marry a girl, he could ask her to be his wife by way of a hand-in-marriage letter, or *carta de pedimento*. A carta de pedimento was initiated by the boy's parents. Of primary importance—and something that was not relaxed until more modern times—was the custom requiring that both sets of parents consent to the marriage; this was sometimes done without consulting with the daughter.

The first step in such a proposal was for the boy's father to send a messenger forewarning the girl's father to expect visitors on a certain date. It was possible, however, for the girl's father to ask the messenger to inform the boy's parents that he did not wish to be asked for his daughter's hand by word of mouth but would rather that the request be made by letter. In many cases, such a letter was hand-carried and delivered by a third party rather than mailed. If neither of the prospective groom's parents knew how to write, the local scribe or someone with writing skills was asked to draft a carta de pedimento.

On occasion, asking for a girl's hand took on a humorous twist. My father and other former residents of the Río Puerco Valley tell of a marriage proposal that involved a ball. The young man would dispense with traditional protocol and simply appear with a ball at the girl's house. Upon opening the front door of their house, he would yell, "¡Bola adentro!" (Here goes the ball!) and threw the ball into the house. Should the ball not be tossed back out, the boy's marriage petition had been granted. If the ball was pitched back out, his marriage proposal was denied. It is not clear who tossed the ball back out, that is, whether it was the girl's father or the girl. This kind of game seems to have occurred between close friends with previously approved marriage arrangements.

The carta de pedimento that follows was donated by Dean L. Campbell, a singer and performer of entriegas (see Chapter 7). Although neither he nor the letter is from the Río Puerco Valley, my interviewees indicate it is representative of those sent by prospective grooms' parents asking for a girl's hand in marriage.

The letter is formal in structure and tone, and the heading, salutation, and closing are serious and decorous. The opening sentence strikes an important chord as it discusses respect and honor, two very important issues in a small community. While the letter is formal, it is not pedantic in its linguistic expression. Instead, a certain tenderness and empathy are conveyed.

HIGINIO GRIEGO WITH DAUGHTERS EREMITA AND CATALINA ON EREMITA'S WEDDING DAY. MARTÍNEZ TOWN, 1946. PHOTO COURTESY OF THE AUTHOR.

CARTA DE PEDIMENTO

Mayo 25, 1919
Ojo del Padre, N.M.
Condado de Sandoval

Señor Horacio Tafoya
Señora Laurencia Tafoya

Apreciados Señores:

Con el más alto respecto y la mayor sumición de su cariño, nos presentamos ante el honor de ustedes, solamente a poner a su conocemiento que nuestro hijo MARIANO él desea con las fibras de su corazón, ponerse en el estado de el santo matrimonio, con su muy estimada señorita ISIDORA. Nosotros como padres de familia y cumpliendo con nuestro dever y la doctrina cristiana y que cumpliendo con nuestros hijos no contrario a su voluntad lo ponemos a conosimiento de ustedes cumpliendo con su dever, lo ponarán al conocimiento de la pretendida señorita ISIDORA para que ella de por sí sola determine lo que sea de Dios su santa voluntad y con eso quedamos esperando su fina resulución.

Sus muy atentos y humildes servidores.

El señor Toribio Romero
La señora Zenaida Montaño de Romero

HAND-IN-MARRIAGE LETTER

May 25, 1919
Ojo del Padre, N.M.
Sandoval County

Mr. Horacio Tafoya
Mrs. Laurencia Tafoya

Dear Friends:

With the utmost respect and the greatest gift of your affection, we come before you and the honor you behold only to apprise you that our son MARIANO wishes with the firmness of his heart to contract in holy matrimony with your beloved daughter ISIDORA. As family parents complying with our duty and the Christian doctrine and thus honoring our obligation to our children, we must award them a status not contrary to their own will. We hereby apprise you of this, thus complying with their duty as well, which you in turn will bring to the attention of your intended daughter ISIDORA so that she of her own accord can determine or let it be God's holy will. With that we await your kind decision.

Your very attentive and humble servants,

Mr. Toribio Romero
Mrs. Zenaida Montaño de Romero

JESÚS CÓRDOVA, DISABLED WORLD WAR I VETERAN, AND HIS WIFE PERFILIA CÓRDOVA, C. 1925. PHOTO COURTESY OF THE AUTHOR.

CARTA DE PADRINOS —
GODPARENTS' MATRIMONY LETTER

Once a girl's parents consented to a marriage, plans for choosing *padrinos* (best man and bride's maid) began, but first came the engagement party, or *prendorio*. Before the prendorio was celebrated, the groom and his parents visited the bride and her parents. The meeting was no doubt formal and perhaps tense, especially if communication up to that point had been by letter. It was during such a visit that the engagement party date was decided. Also, preliminary and sometimes final decisions regarding the padrinos were made at this meeting. Both sets of parents usually decided this matter in consultation with the bride and groom, who were expected to agree with their parents' decision even if their advice had not been sought.

The best man and bride's maid were then asked to act as sponsors at the wedding. This was done either in person or by letter. If the padrinos were not family members, or if they resided in a neighboring village or far away, a *carta de padrinos*, or godparents' letter, came into play. The following carta de padrinos was signed and possibly drafted jointly by the bride and groom's parents. In the letter, they ask a couple to be the nuptial godparents at their daughter and son's wedding. This letter has an interesting feature: Given the date of the letter, the wedding date is only six days later; in all probability, arrangements had been hitherto agreed upon. This letter was then a mere formality. Also worth noting is the fact that only the fathers' names are included, underscoring the males' dominance in these matters.

CARTA DE PADRINOS

San Luis, N.M.
Nov. 21, 1915

Don Felix Lovato y Florinda J. Lovato:

Apreciables señores con toda entegridad y el más alto respeto. Nos presentamos delante de sus mercedes para poner en conocimiento de Uds. que nuestros hijos Genoveba Jaramillo y Federico Lovato entre ambas boluntades Dios les ha dictado elejir a Uds. como padrinos para que los presenten delante al altar de nuestra Santa Madre la Iglecia Católica Apostólica Romana en donde serán unidos en los hindolubles lasos del Santo Matrimonio el Día 27 de Nov. de 1915 por lo cual esperamos de Uds. una decisión faborable y nos repetimos de Uds. sus humildes serbidores a sus ordenes.

Selso Jaramillo y Esposa
José Lovato y Esposa

GODPARENTS' MATRIMONY LETTER

San Luis, N.M.
Nov. 21, 1915

Mr. Felix Lovato and Florinda J. Lovato:

My dear friends, with all integrity and the utmost of respect. We come before your merciful souls in order to apprise you that our children Genoveba Jaramillo and Federico Lovato have agreed through God's will to select you as godparents so that you may present them before the altar of Our Holy Mother, the Roman Catholic Church, where they shall be united in the inseparable bonds of matrimony on the 27th day of November 1915. We hereby await a favorable decision from you and thus reaffirm that we as your humble servants are at your service.

Selso Jaramillo and Wife
José Lovato and Wife

EDUARDO CHÁVEZ, GUADALUPE, N.M., DATE UNKNOWN. PHOTO COURTESY OF
LUCIANO AND MARÍA SÁNCHEZ.

CARTA DE RECHAZO — REJECTION LETTER

In the Río Puerco Valley there was no specified time frame within which the girl's father or parents were to answer the carta de pedimento, although fifteen days was generally acceptable. If the answer was no, the boy was victim of a custom called "getting squashed," or receiving *calabazas* (pumpkins). People would say *"Le dieron calabazas,"* which means "He got squashed." With the boy's ego crushed and his father's pride hurt, all hopes for marriage collapsed. Several interviewees informed me that on such an occasion the girl's mother, moved by pity for the boy, would sometimes put pastries outside the door for the rejected suitor. In that way the boy would not go home empty-handed.

Typically, the girl's father, and sometimes both her parents, dealt the "squashing." The girl's parents, especially her father, usually knew whom they wanted for a son-in-law. In that respect they played an active role as go-betweens in ensuring that their wishes were met. Their daughter's wishes, while important, were generally of secondary significance and hence were superseded by tradition.

The following *carta de rechazo*, or rejection letter, represents an intriguing case in which the girl, not the father, doled out the pumpkins. It was drafted and sent to her fiancé for reasons outlined in the communication. Anger, love, and compassion are all mentioned, but, more importantly, the letter reveals that her pride and independence underlie her unwillingness to be the suitor's second choice. Given the inordinate number of misspelled words, the lack of punctuation, and the long run-on sentences, it is obvious that this is not the work of a scribe but of a girl inspired by her emotions. The letter's grammatical shortcomings do not detract from its substance for it contains coherent and heartfelt thoughts that no scribe could have composed. It is our misfortune that the sender and the recipient's names were not included in the transcribed material donated for this book; however, the writer's spirited response says far more than any appellation could possibly suggest.

CARTA DE RECHAZO

Angostura, N.M.
11 de Noviembre de 1899

Señor Don—mi muy querido y apreciable joven que yo aprecio. Esta es con el solo fin de saludarte y decirte que lla no es mi boluntad de casarme contigo, porque me dijeron que abías dicho tú que ybas apedir mujer en La Tijera [San Luis] y que sino te daban benías aperdirme amí pero dejate de eso porque no estoy afaltas tullas ni de nadien gracias a Dios que nada ay perdido en eso bibo en grida en el mundo y tu lo sabes megor que para mí no abía más cielo que tú en quien tenías puestos mis ojos pero el quererte y amarte es aparte y el que quieras que llo baste es otra cosa y yo no tengo nececidá de sufrir tanto por que mejor lo dirán todas las gentes que llo no me doy ese trato pues querido—llo te agradesco mucho la buena boluntad que me mostrabas tu amí. Esta es la última boluntad de tu querida llo te sintería mucho de ti esto por que llo te amaba mucho y por mi no te con muebas y no más por ora así asen los hombres de bien cuando quedan bien.

CARTA DE RECHAZO – REJECTION LETTER

Angostura, N.M.

11 November 1899

Dear Mr.—my very dear and beloved young man whom I admire. This letter is with the sole intent of greeting you and informing you that it is no longer my desire to marry you, because I have been informed that you had said that you were going to ask for a girl's hand in marriage in La Tijera [San Luis] and if unsuccessful then you would resort to me, but forget it for I'm neither your fool or anyone else's. Thanks be to God that nothing's been lost, for you know that I live proudly on this earth, although I have known you better than anyone [and] that for me there was no one else but you for whom I had eyes, but loving you and caring for you is another matter. I don't have any need to suffer like that, and who's a better witness than the people who know that I don't deserve that treatment. Well dear—I appreciate the good will you showed toward me. This in turn is the last show of affection from your sweetheart. I feel sorry for you because I loved you very much, but as for me, don't worry. After all that's what men of good will do in order to remain in good standing.

NASARIO P. GARCÍA AND AGAPITA LÓPEZ ON THEIR WEDDING DAY. JUNE 17, 1935, BERNALILLO, N.M. PHOTO COURTESY OF THE AUTHOR.

THE SAN LUIS GONZAGA CHURCH, SAN LUIS, N.M., 1995. PHOTO BY THE AUTHOR.

LIBERATO AND ANTOÑITA LEYBA ON THEIR WEDDING DAY, JUNE 6, 1924, ALGODONES, N.M. PHOTO COURTESY OF RITA LEYBA LAST.

CHAPTER 7

ENTRIEGAS

DELIVERIES

IN THE MATRIX OF HISPANIC FOLKLORE IN NORTHERN NEW MEXICO, there are only two kinds of *entriegas,* or songs that are spoken or sung. The word *entriega* derives from the verb *entregar,* which means to deliver or to hand over. *Entriega* in this case is used as a noun, *la entriega.* An *entriega de novios* was either recited or sung to celebrate the presentation of a newly wedded couple to the community, and an *entriega de bautismo* concurred with the delivery of a newly christened infant to his parents. More than anything else, an entriega de bautismo symbolized a lifetime commitment among four fundamental entities: the Church, the godparents, the coparents, and the *(a)hijada/o,* or godchild.

Entriegas de novios are indigenous to New Mexico. Juan B. Rael wrote many years ago about entriegas de novios: "Of all the ceremonies that take place during the typical New Mexican Spanish wedding, the *entrega de novios* is perhaps the most genuinely New Mexican."[1] Rael pointed out, however, that "the singing of *coplas* [a short one-stanza poem in eight-syllable verses that treats an array of popular themes] at weddings or apropos of an approaching marriage is found in Spain." He contends, though, that however slight the resemblance in some of the stanzas, it is probably more happenstance than outright imitation.

ENTRIEGA DE BAUTISMO — BAPTISMAL DELIVERY

On baptism day, after the godparents had made arrangements with the priest and perhaps with the church caretaker, several activities occurred. The day's events started with a Mass and baptism at church and ended with a family fiesta at either the parents' or one of the grandparents' homes. On this day, the padrinos delivered the layette, or *canastilla*, which everyone had eagerly awaited. The godmother alone dressed the child, and seeing the baby dressed for his baptism was very special. The godparents then collected the child from his parents' home and took the baby to church. During the christening ceremony, the godparents supplied the priest with the child's name or names, and then the child was baptized. After the christening, the priest filled out the certificate of baptism that identified the child and his sponsors, that is, his parents and godparents, by name. The priest then signed the certificate, and the information was entered into the church's Baptismal Register.

Upon returning to the infant's home, the now-official godparents delivered the child to his parents with the recitation of an entriega. The verses underscore the bond between the *compadres* (father and godfather) and the *comadres* (mother and godmother), and they acknowledge the fulfillment of the parents and godparents' duties. These verses that follow were made available by Eduardo Valdez.

Compadre, comadre
aquí está esta fresca rosa
con los Santos Sacramentos
y l'gua que recibió.

Compadre, comadre
we bring you this fresh rose
blessed with the Holy Sacraments
and the holy water it was blessed with.

The child's parents usually responded with a verse such as this:

Recibimos esta rosa fresca
que de la iglesia salites
con los Santos Sacramentos
y l'agua que recibites.

We accept this fresh rose
who exited the church
blessed with the Holy Sacraments
as well as the holy water it received.

Congratulations were offered, perhaps accompanied by a toast, *un brinde*, then a fiesta followed. Guests, relatives, and sometimes close friends and neighbors attended the celebration, which was replete with food, pastry, and drinks.

ENTRIEGA DE NOVIOS —
DELIVERY OF THE BRIDE AND GROOM

Weddings were very important because of their religious importance and their social enjoyment. Whether of the rich or of the poor, they were joyous affairs. A wedding day's activities began early in the morning, starting with Mass around nine o'clock, and ended late that evening, or many times as late as dawn the next day, following a dance. Before the wedding ceremony took place, the comadres-to-be, the bride and groom's mothers, dressed the bride at her parents' home. The groom dressed at his own home or at a relative's house near the church. Then, all the principals gathered at the church.

The bride and groom and their families, having fasted the night before, went to confession and received Communion, as did everyone else. During the much-anticipated wedding ceremony, the bride and groom received the sacrament of matrimony and a few words of advice from the priest; the Mass ended soon thereafter.

Following the church ceremony, the newlyweds, their families, the godparents, and guests went to the bride's home or to the community dance hall, where the wedding fiesta was celebrated.

During the reception, there was much conversation and music, as well as singing, dancing, and drinking, which was interrupted only by the entriega de novios. This was an important event, and it was when the bride and groom were handed over, or *entregados*, as man and wife to families and friends in the community.

As a child, I recall the entriega being celebrated shortly after the big meal had been served. An *entregador*, rarely an *entregadora* it appears, sang the entriega. In some cases he was the local poet; in others, he was a family friend. Nevertheless, he was adept at composing on the spot new verses that suited the newlyweds. During the recitation, the entregador played a guitar, and while he usually sang alone, he was sometimes accompanied by a violinist or other musician. During the entriega, the bride and groom faced the entregador and everyone else formed a circle around them. The entregador then sang his song.

Many times the entregador did not charge for his services. If he did charge, he collected from the people while he sang. The money was collected during the entriega by passing a hat or dish among the people encircling the couple and the entregador; sometimes coins were tossed onto a bedsheet on the floor. If the entregador had been paid beforehand or if he was performing the entriega for free, he gave the donated money to the couple to help them start a new life.

The entriegas that follow are similar in structure, form, and rhyme, although inconsistencies may be found in all three areas. The four- and sometimes six-line verses have eight-syllable lines, with assonance on the second and fourth verses (*memOriA/ glOriA*, and *purEzA/promEsA*). The number of stanzas ranges from a few to more than twenty. In all entriegas de novios, there are two messages for the newly conjoined man and wife: Heed the sacrament of matrimony and uphold the spiritual and moral obligations of marriage for their sake as well as that of their children.

Today, entriegas are heard at weddings throughout New Mexico, and although they are rarely presented by a traditional entregador, they are performed by several musicians playing string and wind instruments and sometimes by a band.

VICENTITA CHÁVEZ

Entriega de novios

I

*"Ave María" dijo 'lave
para empezar a volar.
Y "Ave María" digo yo
para empezar a cantar.*

II

*Atención pido atención
a los que han acompañado.
Para que oigan estos versos
de los recién esposados.*

The Delivery of Bride and Groom

I

"Holy Mary," said the bird
before starting to fly.
And "Holy Mary," say I
before starting to sing.

II

Attention is what I request
from those who are present.
So that you'll hear these verses
dedicated to the newlyweds.

III

Para empezar a cantar
a Dios le pido memoria.
Pa que les conceda estos
novios
como a San Pedro en
la Gloria.

IV

El padre les preguntó
si se querían casar.
Y la Iglesia les oyó
el acto matrimonial.

V

La novia con traje blanco
demostrando la pureza.
Se presenta en el templo
para cumplir su promesa.

VI

Con una hermosa corona
de blancas flores de azar.
Se presenta a recibir
al anillo conyugal.

VII

¿Qué senifican las velas
cuando las van a prender?
Senifica [n] el mismo cuerpo
que ya va permanecer.

VIII

Las arras² que les echaron
a los esposos queridos.
Y el yugo conyugal
que el Señor ha requerido.

IX

Durante la santa misa
con cuatro velas veladas.
Para que vivan felices
El Señor las ha alumbrado.

III

In order to start singing
I ask God's help in remembering.
So God may grant this couple
a blessing as He did St. Peter
in Heaven.

IV

The priest asked them both
if they wanted to get married.
And the Church heard them
through the marriage ceremony.

V

The bride, in a white dress,
shows off her purity.
She goes to the altar
ready to fulfill her promise.

VI

With a beautiful crown
made from white, happy flowers.
She presents herself to receive
the conjugal ring.

VII

What do the candles symbolize
when they're about to be lit?
They symbolize the same body
that's going to persist.

VIII

The coins² cast upon them
the beloved husband and wife.
And the nuptial ties
that Christ has demanded.

IX

During the holy mass
with four lit candles.
So that they burn happily
Christ our Lord has lit them.

X

En este dichoso día
en el templo religioso.
La novia con traje blanco
recibe a su amado esposo.

XI

De la iglesia vi salir
un arco con cuatro rosas.
El padrino y la madrina
y el esposo con su esposa.

XII

¡Qué bonitas son las flores
tejidas con verdes ramas!
¡Qué lindos se ven los novios
sentados junto a los damas!

XIII

Les dieron buenos consejos
a sus queridos hijados.
Que cumplan con su deber
como buenos esposados.

XIV

Demos un voto de gracia
a los que nos han honrado.
En sacramento tan gusto
y nos han acompañado.

XV

A la recién esposada
suplico lo que es debido.
Ya no hay padre, ya no
hay madre
'hora lo que hay es marido.

X

On this fortuitous day
at the religious temple.
The bride, in her white dress,
takes the groom for a husband.

XI

From the church I saw departing
an arch with four red roses.
The godfather and godmother
and the husband and wife.

XII

How beautiful are the flowers
interwoven with green branches!
How beautiful the couple looks
seated next to the maids
of honor!

XIII

The dear, beloved godchildren
were given sound advice.
May they comply with their duty
like every good husband
and wife.

XIV

Let us give thanks
to those who have honored us.
In such a happy sacrament
they have accompanied us.

XV

Of the newly wedded wife
I ask what's duty bound.
Now there is no father or mother
what now exists is a husband.

XVI

Oygame Ud. el esposado
lo que le voy a esplicar.
Esta cruz que Dios le ha dado
no la valla abandonar.

XVII

Si deja su cruz por otra
ella pegará un suspiro.
Y Ud. será responsable
en el Tribunal Divino.

XVIII

Si cumplen con su deber
mi Dios los debe premiar.
Que el esposo con su esposa
al cielo deven entrar.

XIX

El esposado y la esposa
que vivan con alegría.
¡Qué sean buenos casados
como San José y María!

XX

Del patriarca San José
y de su esposa María.
Procuren seguir su ejemplo
y estarán en su companía.

XXI

Ya los padrinos queridos
van a cumplir su deber.
Van a entregar sus hijados
con un fino proceder.

XXII

Entre suegros y consuegras
no debe de haber enojos.
Porque se van a juntar
las dos niñas de sus ojos.

XVI

Listen to me dear husband
hear what I'm about to explain.
This cross that God has given
you
don't you dare abandon it.

XVII

If you forsake her for another
she will let out a sigh.
And you shall have to answer
to the Divine Tribunal.

XVIII

If both comply with your duty
my dear God will reward you.
For the husband and wife
shall enter heaven hand in hand.

XIX

May husband and wife
live in happiness.
May they be good in marriage
like St. Joseph and Mary!

XX

From the patriarch St. Joseph
and from his wife, Mary.
Try to follow their example
and you shall be in good company.

XXI

The beloved godparents already
are about to fulfill their duty.
By giving away their godchildren
with a delicate demeanor.

XXII

Among all of the in-laws
there must be no bitterness.
Because two eyes' pupils
are about to unite with one
another.

XXIII

Bajo del sol deslumbrante
bajo del cielo divino.
Digan toditos que viva
pues que viva este padrino.

XXIV

A veses miro pasar
las nubes muy cristalinas.
Digan toditos que viva
pues que viva esta madrina.

XXV

No soy trovador ni pueta
no tengo ninguna gracia.
Sólo compongo versitos
cuando son para mi raza.

XXVI

A los padres d'estos novios
sólo me queda decir.
Aquí tienen a sus hijos
ya los pueden recibir.

XXVII

Ya con ésta me despido
humilde y ya bien cansado.
Si en algo me he equivocado
espero ser perdonado.

XXVIII

El que me mandó cantar
hice lo que me mandó.
Acábase de cantar
pero de servirles no.

XXIII

Underneath the glittering sun
underneath the divine sky.
May you all say, "Long live,
long live the godfather."

XXIV

At times I see sailing by
the very clear clouds in the sky.
May you all say, "Long live,
long live the godmother."

XXV

I'm neither a troubadour nor
a poet
I have neither knack nor talent.
I only compose short verses
when they are for my people.

XXVI

To the parents of this couple
I have only one thing to say.
Here are your children
now you may greet them.

XXVII

With this delivery I depart
very tired but quite humbled.
If I have erred in something
I hope to be forgiven.

XXVIII

As for he who asked me to sing
I did just as he requested.
I have just finished singing
but not in serving you.

EDUMENIO LOVATO

Entriega de novios

I

Atención pido a la gente
y a todo este público honrado.
Para celebrar el auto
de estos recién casados.

II

Quisiera tener palabras
como el mejor delegado.
Para poderme explicar
ante este público honrado.

III

En el nombre de Dios comienzo
y en el nombre de la
Virgen María.
Para entregar este estado
que se ha llegado este día.

IV

El sacerdote les preguntó
que si querían matrimoniarse.
Y la Iglesia les oyó
ambos deseo de casarse.

V

El padre con su manual
les explica las palabras.
Y les entriega las arras
y el anillo conjugal.

VI

Ya el haber tomado las arras
y el anillo conjugal.
Es una prueba paterna
es un matrimonio legal.

The Delivery of the Bride and Groom

I

I ask for peoples' attention
and that of this honorable
audience.
In order to celebrate the ritual
of this newly wed couple.

II

I would like to have words
like the best of delegates.
In order to explain myself
before this honorable audience.

III

I begin in the name of God
and in the name of the
Virgin Mary.
In order to deliver this couple
who has arrived on this date.

IV

The priest asked them
if they wanted to get married.
And the Church heard
them express
their desire to do so.

V

The priest, with his missal,
explains the words to them.
And hands the couple the
small coins
as well as the conjugal ring.

VI

Having received the coins
and the conjugal ring.
It is a paternal truth
it is a legal marriage.

VII

Esto no es para un rato
ni para un día o dos.
Es para una eternidad
mientras vivan los dos.

VIII

Dígame el recién casado
lo que le voy hacer saber.
Ya no hay padre ni madre
ahora lo que hay es mujer.

IX

Dígame la recién casada
escúcheme y ponga sentido.
Ya no hay padre ni madre
ahora lo que hay es marido.

X

Dígame el recién casado
lo que le voy amonestar.
Esa cruz que Dios le ha dado
no la vaya abandonar.

XI

Si deja la Cruz por otra
ha de pegar un suspiro.
Ud. ha de ser responsable
a un Tribunal Divino.

XII

Piensan los malos casados
a mi Dios abandonar.
Como cuatro velas veladas
en la misa del altar.

VII

This is not for a brief time
nor for a day or two.
It is for eternity
as long as you both shall live.

VIII

May the new husband tell me
what I'm about to let you know.
There is no longer a father
or mother
what now exists is a wife.

IX

May the new wife tell me
listen to me and use good sense.
There is no longer a father
or mother
what now exists is a husband.

X

May the new husband remember
this admonishment.
Don't you dare abandon
that cross that God has
given you.

XI

If you forsake this cross
for another
you must give out a sigh.
You will have to answer
to the Divine Tribunal.

XII

To abandon the marriage
is to abandon God.
Like ignoring during the mass
four burning candles.

XIII

Y ya de la iglesia ha salido
esperando con gran fe.
Dios les haga buenos casados
como Santa María y
San José.

XIV

Ahora son esposados
en este dichoso día.
Ya son recién casados
como San José y
Santa María.

XV

De lo profundo del cielo
corre el agua cristalina.
De donde se lavan las manos
el padrino y la madrina.

XVI

Muy de mañana salieron
de la iglesia cuatro rosas.
El padrino y la madrina
el esposo y su esposa.

XVII

El padrino y la madrina
ya saben su obligación.
De entregar a sus hijados
y echales su bendición.

XVIII

A los padres de estos novios
les expreso mi cariño.
Que reciban a sus hijos
y les den el buen camino.

XIX

Ya la entriega se ha acabado
y la honra queda encendida.
Señoras y caballeros
dispensen lo mal servido.

XIII

Once you have left the church
and are relying on great faith.
May God make you a good
husband and wife
like St. Mary and St. Joseph.

XIV

Now they have been united
on this fortuitous day.
You are now newlyweds
like St. Joseph and St. Mary.

XV

Underneath the divine sky
runs crystal clear water.
Where the godfather and
godmother
wash their hands.

XVI

Very early they came out
four roses from the church.
The godfather and godmother
and the husband and wife.

XVII

The godfather and godmother
already know of their duty.
To deliver their godchildren
and to give them their blessing.

XVIII

To the parents of this couple
I express my affection.
May they receive their children
and wish them well on their way.

XIX

The delivery is now over
and the flame of honor lit.
Ladies and gentlemen
forgive me for my shortcomings.

EDUARDO VALDEZ

Entriega de novios

I

Para empezar a cantar
ante este público honrado.
Para festejar el auto
de los recién esposados.

II

A todo resto de casa
escuchen les voy hablar.
Si en algo me equivocare
me deben de dispensar.

III

Para empezar a cantar
a Dios le pido memoria.
Que les conceda a
estos novios
como a San Pedro en la gloria.

IV

Fueron a tomarse el dicho
estando los dos allí.
El padre les preguntó
ambos dos dijieron sí.

V

El padre les preguntó
si se querían casar.
Y la Iglesia los oyó
en auto matrimonial.

VI

A las ocho de la mañana
se fueron a presentar.
A la madre que es la Iglesia
no la vayan a engañar.

The Delivery of Bride and Groom

I

In order to begin singing
before this honorable audience.
To begin to celebrate the ritual
of the recently married.

II

To the rest of you present
listen to what I'm going to say.
Should I err in something
I ask for your forgiveness.

III

In order to begin singing
I ask God's help in remembering.
May He grant this couple
a blessing
as He did with St. Peter
in Heaven.

IV

The two of them standing there
celebrating their vows.
The priest asked them both
and they responded yes.

V

The priest asked them both
if they wanted to marry.
And the Church heard them
through the marriage ceremony.

VI

At eight o'clock in the morning
they went to present themselves.
To the Mother who is the Church
so don't go and deceive Her.

VII

En el cuerpo de la iglesia
un sacerdote decía.
Tienen que ser esposados
como San José y María.

VIII

¿Qué significan las velas
cuando las van a prender?
Significan el mismo cuerpo
que ya va permanecer.

IX

¿Qué significan las velas
cuando las van apagar?
Significan el matrimonio
y el anillo pastoral.

X

Hizo Dios con su poder
Adán con sabiduría.
Y le sacó una costilla
y de allí formó a la mujer.

XI

Hizo que Adán durmiera
en un hermoso vergel.
Y le dio una compañera
que se estuviera con él.

XII

Ya vuelve Adán de su sueño
con voz muy admirable.
Te recibo por esposa
por obedecer al Padre.

VII

In the body of the church
a priest was advising.
You must be husband and wife
like St. Joseph and Mary.

VIII

What do the candles signify
when they're about to be lit?
They symbolize the very same
body
that is going to become one.

IX

What do the candles signify
when they're about to be put out?
They symbolize matrimony
and the pastoral ring.

X

God created with His power
Adam, who possessed
knowledge.
And from him God extracted
a rib
from which He made a woman.

XI

He made Adam go to sleep
in a beautiful flower garden.
And He gave him a mate
so that she'd be with him.

XII

Adam returns from his dream
with a very melodious voice.
I take you for my wife
in obedience to the Lord.

XIII
Muy de mañana salieron
de la iglesia cuatro rosas.
El padrino y la madrina
el esposo con su esposa.

XIV
Ya salieron de la iglesia
en este dichoso día.
Ya salieron esposados
como San José y María.

XV
Ya llegaron los padrinos
en este dichoso día.
Con sus ahijados a un lado
como San José y María.

XVI
El sacramento divino
tan blanco como una rosa.
Viva Manuel López
manifestando su esposa.

XVII
Escuche usted el esposado
no crea que por mandar.
Esa cruz que Dios le ha dado
no la vaya a abandonar.

XVIII
Si deja su cruz por otra
ella pegará un suspiro.
Y usted será responsable
ante el Tribunal Divino.

XIX
Escucha tu palomita
escucha y pon buen sentido.
Ya no hay padre, ya no
hay madre
ahora lo que hay es marido.

XIII
Very early they exited the church
four beautiful red roses
The godfather and godmother
and the husband and wife.

XIV
They've already exited
the church
on this fortuitous day.
They've left married
like St. Joseph and Mary.

XV
The godparents have arrived
on this fortuitous day.
Their godchildren at their side
like St. Joseph and Mary.

XVI
The divine sacrament
as white as a rose.
Long live Manuel López
who shows off his wife.

XVII
Listen, my new husband
don't think of yourself as boss.
Don't you dare abandon
the cross God has given you.

XVIII
If you abandon her for another
she will let out a sigh.
And you will have to answer
to a Divine Tribunal.

XIX
Listen my little pigeon
and pay close attention.
There is no longer a father
or mother
now there is only a husband.

XX

No crean que por mandar
en este punto verlos.
Si nuestros padres dan crianza.
Naturales sólo Dios.

XXI

Bajo ese cielo divino
corre l'agua cristalina.
Donde se lavan las manos
el padrino y la madrina.

XXII

El padrino y la madrina
ya saben su obligación.
De entregar a sus ahijados
que reciban la bendición.

XXIII

A los padres de estos novios
sólo me queda decir.
Aquí tienen a sus hijos
ya los pueden recibir.

XXIV

De mi parte les diré
si soy digno de atención.
Hínquense los esposados
reciban la bendición.

XXV

Entre suegros y consuegros
manifiesten la verdad.
Que en este dichoso día
han cambiado voluntad.

XX

Don't think that from
this moment forward
you are your own bosses.
Sure, our parents raise us
but only God can give
us children.

XXI

Underneath the divine sky
runs crystal clear water.
Where godfather and godmother
both wash their hands.

XXII

The godfather and godmother
already know their duty.
To present their godchildren
so they may receive
their blessings.

XXIII

To the parents of this couple
there is only one thing to say.
Here are your children
you may now receive them.

XXIV

As for me I shall tell you
if I may have your attention.
May the newlyweds kneel
so that you may be blessed.

XXV

Among all of the in-laws
let the truth be known.
On this fortuitous day
you have agreed to wills
of sorts.

XXVI

Entre suegros y consuegros
no deben haber enojos.
Porque se van a juntar
las dos niñas de sus ojos.

XXVII

El que me mandó cantar
sé lo que me mandó.
Acabaré de cantar
pero de servirle no.

XXVIII

Aquí acabo de cantar
ya con ésta me despido.
A todos les doy las gracias
dispensen lo mal servido.

XXVI

Among all of the in-laws
there must not be any anger.
Because two sets of eyes.
are about to be united.

XXVII

As for he who asked me to sing
I know what he requested.
I shall finish singing
but not in serving him.

XXVIII

Here's where my singing ends
with this song I bid farewell.
I thank everyone and
ask you to forgive me if I've not
served you well.

NOTES

1. Juan B. Rael, "New Mexican Wedding Songs," *Southern Folklore Quarterly*, 4 (June 1940): 55.

2. *Arras*, according to Rubén Cobos, are "thirteen small coins which the groom gives to his bride as a pledge of his willingness to support her." *A Dictionary of New Mexico and Southern Colorado Spanish* (Santa Fe: Museum of New Mexico Press, 1983), 12.

BROTHERS JOSÉ TAFOYA AND LUIS TAFOYA, TWO POPULAR MUSICIANS IN
GUADALUPE, NM. DATE OF PHOTO UNKNOWN. COURTESY OF INESITA
MÁREZ-TAFOYA.

CHAPTER 8

CANCIONES

SONGS

The legacy of Hispanic music in New Mexico began with the arrival of Juan de Oñate and his entourage in 1598. It is believed that *alabados*, or hymns of praise, were first sung in New Mexico at the time of his arrival. Subsequently, a number of church representatives, among them members of the Franciscan order, brought and introduced their own church music and musical instruments to the Indians in some of the pueblos along the Río Grande. Among these Franciscans was Bernardo de Mata, a Spaniard who ventured to the New World and eventually ended up in New Mexico around 1605.[1] He played the organ and taught music to the Indians. He died in 1635 at Zía Pueblo, west of the Río Grande northwest of Bernalillo. Friar Juan de San Francisco y Zúñiga in 1630 took charge of the San Antonio de Artiaga Mission south of Socorro, where he installed an organ. He taught the Piró Indians music as well, and he died in 1673 in Senecú.

Of the musical instruments that were to come into New Mexico, the guitar by far has been the most popular. It was introduced from Spain via Mexico and was central to the important role music would have during the next 450 years. Little by little other instruments such as the still-popular violin and the accordion, both of European origin, gained influence in many Hispanic villages. Over time, the harmonica and mandolin, also of European origin, and the banjo made their way into New Mexico. With the exception of the banjo, all of these instruments are used by Hispanic musicians today. The *guitarrón*, a bass stringed instrument indigenous to Mexico, is used today by New Mexican mariachi bands.

Throughout the history of New Mexico, music, like religion and language itself, has comprised a major part of the Hispanic culture. Regardless of the rugged life that settlers experienced, they made time for musical entertainment. The religious calendar, with its many saints' days, provided an outlet for merrymaking and enjoyment in the villages.

Over the centuries, virtually every social engagement—be it solemn or gay, sacred or secular—involved music. Religious songs, ranging from alabados (see Chapter 9) to other songs popular at Christmas, baptisms, and weddings, have long been an integral part of Northern New Mexico's musical heritage.

One type of popular song that existed in Hispanic New Mexican villages was the *romance*, or ballad (see Chapter 4). There was also a more modern popular love song, or *canción*, which made its way from Mexico into different parts of New Mexico.

We must bear in mind that folk songs are susceptible to change. This is especially true of their structure and of their lyrics.

Hence, one finds some variations of the same song even within a community. Around 1978, some twenty years after the demise of the last village of the Río Puerco Valley, popular songs I knew as a child were but vague memories in people's minds. At best, former residents could recall titles or short verses and sometimes hum a song's tune. Titles such as *"Rincón de Marcos," "La Rielera," "Zenaida,"* and *"El Venadito,"* had vanished completely from their minds. Only one or two people I interviewed had ever owned an instrument. Samuel Córdova said he played the violin *a rasguños*, that is, by scratching on it. He and former valley residents recalled the names of different types of dances, such as *la cuna, el cutilio, el chotis, la cuadrilla, el rechumbé, la raspa, el redondo*, and what they called *la varsoliana*. There were also polkas and waltzes that older people once danced to. The following are children's songs, popular songs, and religious songs that were heard in the Río Puerco Valley from the 1930s through the 1950s.

CANCIONES DE NIÑOS — CHILDREN'S SONGS

Children's songs were popular when I started elementary school in Rincón del Cochino, which lies between Guadalupe and Casa Salazar. We sang some songs in English; others we sang in Spanish. My teacher taught us *"Naranja dulce,"* or "Sweet Little Orange," when I was in the first or second grade.

Naranja dulce	Sweet Little Orange
Naranja dulce,	Sweet little orange,
limón partido.	poor sour lemon.
Dame un besito,	Give me a sweet kiss,
que yo te pido.	that I beg of you.

No son falsos,
mis pensamientos.
Yo te aseguro,
que yo no miento.

My only thoughts,
are not false.
I can assure you,
that I don't lie.

Naranja dulce,
limón partido.
Tú no te sabes,
lo que he sufrido.

Sweet little orange,
poor sour lemon.
You don't know
how I've suffered.

Si mis pensamientos
te fueran falsos,
pues ya hace tiempo,
me hubieras dicho.

If my thoughts
were lies,
long ago,
you'd have told me.

YOUNG BOYS IN VILLAGE OF GUADALUPE, 1938. PHOTO BY
PAUL ALFRED FRANCIS WALTER, JR.

CANCIONES POPULARES — POPULAR SONGS

Many songs, most of which were of Mexican origin, were played on the radio during the 1940s. In addition to other songs, my mother sang corridos such as *"Rosita Alvírez,"* which was popular in Guadalupe, as well as *"Cielito lindo"* and *"Allá en el rancho grande."*

Rosita Alvírez

El año mil nuevecientos
treinta y cinco,
presento lo tengo yo.
Jue el año cuando
Rosita Alvírez murió,
Rosita Alvírez murió.

Su mamá se lo dicía,
—Esta noche no me sales.
—Mamá no tengo la culpa,
que a mí me gusten los bailes,
que a mí me gusten los bailes.

Llegó este muchacho al baile,
y a Rosita se derigió.
Como era la más bonita,
Rosita lo desaigró,
Rosita lo desaigró.

—Rosita no me desaigres,
la gente lo va notar,
la gente lo va notar.
—A mí no me importa nada,
contigo no he de bailar,
contigo no he de bailar.

Echó mano a la cintura
y una pistola sacó.
Y a la pobre de Rosita,
no más tres tiros le dio,
no más tres tiros le dio.

Rosita Alvírez

It was the year 1935,
I still recall it well.
It was the year when
Rosita Alvírez died,
when Rosita Alvírez died.

Her mother had admonished her,
"Tonight you're not going out."
"Mom, it's not my fault I
like dances,
it's not my fault I like dances."

This boy got to the dance,
and he headed for Rosita.
Since she was the prettiest,
Rosita turned him down,
Rosita turned him down.

"Rosita, don't rebuff me,
what will people say,
what will people say?"
"I don't care one bit, but
with you I will not dance,
with you I will not dance."

He put his hand on his waist,
and took out a pistol.
And poor little Rosita,
was shot three times,
was shot three times.

Cielito lindo

De la Sierra Morena,
cielito lindo,
viene bajando,
un par de ojitos negros,
cielito lindo,
de contrabando.

Ay, ay, ay, ay.
Canta y no llores,
porque cantando se alegran
cielito lindo los corazones.

Ese lunar que tienes
cielito lindo
junto a la boca,
no se lo des a naide
cielito lindo
que a mí me toca.

Ay, ay, ay, ay.
Canta y no llores,
porque cantanto se alegran
cielito lindo los corazones.

Allá en el rancho grande

Allá en el rancho grande
allá donde vivía.
Había una rancherita,
que alegre merecía
que alegre merecía.

Te voy hacer unos calzones,
como los que usa el ranchero.
Te los comienzo de lana,
y te los acabo de cuero.

Beautiful Little Sky

From the Sierra Morena,
my beautiful little sky,
is descending,
a pair of little dark eyes,
my beautiful little sky,
by way of contraband.

Oh, oh, oh, oh.
Sing and don't cry,
because singing makes the
heart happy
my beautiful little sky.

That mole that you have,
my beautiful little sky
close to your mouth,
don't give it to anyone,
my beautiful little sky,
because it belongs to me.

Oh, oh, oh, oh.
Sing and don't cry,
because singing makes the
heart happy
my beautiful little sky.

There at the Big Ranch

There at the big ranch,
where I used to live.
There lived a young cowgirl,
who was happy as could be,
who was happy as could be.

I'm going to make you a
pair of pants
like the ones that
the rancher wears.
I'll make them from wool
and I'll finish them with leather.

Allá en el rancho grande,	There at the big ranch,
allá donde vivía.	where I used to live.
Había una rancherita,	There lived a young cowgirl,
que alegre me lo decía,	who was happy as could be,
que alegre me lo decía.	who was happy as could be.
Te voy a hacer un sombrero,	I'm going to make you a hat,
como el que usa el ranchero.	like the one the rancher wears.
Te lo comienzo redondo	I'll make it round,
y te lo acabo sin fondo.	and I'll finish it without a top.
Allá en el rancho grande,	There at the big ranch,
allá donde vivía.	where I used to live.
Había una rancherita,	There lived a young cowgirl,
que alegre me lo decía,	who was happy as could be,
que alegre me lo decía.	who was happy as could be.
Te voy hacer una camisa	I'm going to make you a shirt,
para que vayas a misa.	so that you'll go to church.
Te la comienzo de lana,	I'll make it from wool,
y te la acabo de pana.	and I'll finish it with corduroy.
Allá en el rancho grande,	There at the big ranch,
allá donde vivía.	where I used to live.
Había una rancherita,	There lived a young cowgirl,
que alegre me lo decía,	who was happy as could be,
que alegre me lo decía.	who was happy as could be.

La Cucaracha*

The Cucaracha*

La Cucaracha,	The Cucaracha,
la Cucaracha,	the Cucaracha,
ya no quiere caminar,	doesn't want to run,
porque no tiene,	because it's missing,
porque le falta,	because it's lacking,
marijuana que fumar.	marihuana to smoke.

* Pancho Villa's jalopy was a 1923 Dodge touring sedan, according to Rubén Cobos. Villa's men named it "La Cucaracha," which literally means "The Cockroach."

Las muchachas de hoy en día
no saben echar una tortilla,
pero no les hablen del bolote,
porque no falta quien
las alborote.

La Cucaracha,
la Cucaracha,
ya no quiere caminar,
porque no tiene,
porque le falta,
marihuana que fumar.

The girls of today,
can't even make tortillas,
but don't tell them about
a dance,
for there's always someone
who can make them prance.

The Cucaracha,
the Cucaracha,
doesn't want to run any more,
because it's missing,
because it's lacking,
marihuana to smoke.

Adelita*

Si Adelita se juera con otro,
la seguiría por tierra
y por mar.
Si por mar en un buque
de guerra,
y por tierra en un tren
militar.

Si toca que yo muera en
la guerra,
y si mi cuerpo en la sierra
va quedar.
Adelita por Dios te lo ruego,
que por mí no vayas a llorar.

Si Adelita quisiera ser
mi esposa,
si Adelita ya juera mi mujer.
Le compraría un vestido
de seda,
antes de llevarla al cuartel.

Adelita*

If Adelita were to leave
with another,
I'd follow her by land or sea.
If by sea, it would be on
a warship,
and by land, it would be on a
military train.

If it turns out that I die in
the war,
and if my body is left in
the mountains.
Adelita, for God's sake, I beg you,
please don't go shed any tears
for me.

If Adelita wished to be my wife,
if Adelita were already mine,
I'd buy her a dress made of silk,
before taking her to my quarters.

---

* A popular song composed during the Mexican Revolution.

Mi chaparrita

Adiós mi chaparrita,
no llores por tu Pancho,
que si se va del rancho,
muy pronto volverá.

Verás que en las tiendas,
te compro buenas prendas.
Y el beso que tú esperas,
muy pronto lo sentirás.

Adiós mi chaparrita,
no llores por tu Pancho,
que si se va del rancho,
muy pronto volverá.

My Sweetheart

Good-bye my sweetheart,
don't cry for your Pancho,
for if he leaves the ranch,
he'll return soon thereafter.

You'll see that in the stores,
I'll buy you fine jewels,
and [as for] the kiss you await,
you'll feel it very soon.

Good-bye my sweetheart,
don't cry for your Pancho,
for if he leaves the ranch,
he'll return soon thereafter.

CANCIONES RELIGIOSAS — RELIGIOUS SONGS

My paternal grandmother once had a church choir in Guadalupe. Many children from the village sang with her, and it was from her that they learned many religious songs. Because I lived far from the church, I learned religious songs from her at her home. The following are songs we sang as children.

Vamos todos a Belén

Vamos todos a Belén,
con amor y gozo.
Adoremos al Señor,
nuestro Redentor.

Relumbra una estrella,
Divino dulzor.
Que bonita y bella,
nuestro Salvador.

Let Us Go to Bethlehem

Let us go to Bethlehem,
with love and joy.
Let us pray to our Lord
Jesus Christ,
our Redeemer.

A star shines brightly,
on our sweet Divine One.
A pretty star shines,
brightly on our Savior.

JOSÉ SÁNCHEZ, BARBER AND MUSICIAN, GUADALUPE VILLAGE. DATE OF PHOTO UNKNOWN.
COURTESY OF LUCIANO AND MARÍA SÁNCHEZ.

Noche de paz

Noche de paz,
noche de amor.
Todos duermen,
en rededor.

Entre los astros,
que esparcen su luz,
van ya anunciando,
al niño Jesús.

Brilla la estrella,
la estrella de paz,
que ya no nos queda,
cosa más bella.

Oh, Peaceful Night

Oh, peaceful night,
oh, peaceful night.
Everyone's asleep.
here and there.

The Stars that shine
their light from above,
are telling us that
Jesus Christ is born.

The Star of Peace
shines brightly,
for nothing more beautiful
is left for us to see.

Bendito, bendito

Bendito, bendito,
bendito sea a Dios.
Los ángeles cantan,
y alaban a Dios.
Los ángeles cantan,
y alaban a Dios.

Yo creo Dios mío,
que estás en el altar.
Oculto en la hostia,
te vengo yo adorar.
Oculto en la hostia,
te vengo yo adorar.

Adoro en la hostia,
el cuerpo del Señor.
Su sangre preciosa,
que dio por mí en la cruz.
Su sangre preciosa,
que dio por mí en la cruz.

Blessed, Oh, Blessed

Blessed, oh, blessed,
oh, blessed, oh, Lord.
The angels are singing,
and praising God.
The angels are singing,
and praising God.

I believe, my dear God,
that you're at the altar.
Disguised as you are in the host,
I have come to pray to you.
Disguised as you are in the host,
I have come to pray to you.

I adore in the host,
the body of our Lord.
His precious blood,
that he sacrificed
for me on the cross.
His precious blood,
that he sacrificed
for me on the cross.

BRUNA VALENCIA MARES

A nuestra madre querida[2]

No hay cosa como la madre
en la vida traicionera,
que la tienes llena de vida,
y Dios se la lleva a la gloria.
Si cuando a sus pies caímos
nos recive de abismo,
con las aguas del Bautismo,
que en el templo recibimos.
Allí nos lleva un compadre,
el cual es nuestro padrino,
pero al guiar nuestro destino,
no hay cosa como la madre.
Puesto que un pesar que da
un hijo,
Dios en el calvario dijo:
—No hay cosa como la madre,
el hijo que madre tiene,
no puede ser desgraciado,
porque Dios ha conservado,
es que le comviene.
Porque la madre querida,
lo colma de bendiciones,
y alivia sus aflicciones,
mientras Dios le presta vida.
Cuando empezamos a andar,
guía nuestros primeros pasos,
teniéndonos de los brazos,
nos comienza a librar.
Con sólo un perro que ladre,
y luego nos alza del suelo,
porque debajo del cielo,
no hay cosa como la madre.

There Is Nothing Like Your Mother[2]

There is nothing like your mother
in this treacherous world,
she who is so full of life
whom God takes to his side.
If we should fall at her feet,
she'll save us from the abyss
as if blessing us with Holy Water
that we received at church.
There we are taken by a friend
who is known as our godfather.
But as for guiding our destiny
there is nothing like your mother.
In spite of some grief a child
may bring,
God said this at Calvary,
"There is nothing like your mother;
a child who has his mother
cannot be considered unfortunate,
for God has saved her
as his servant."
Because the loving mother
will fill him with blessings
and alleviate his afflictions
as long as God grants her life on
this earth.
When we learn to walk,
she guides our first steps.
She guides us firmly by holding
our hand.
She begins to protect us
even from the bark of a dog.
Then she lifts us off the ground,
which reminds us that beneath
the heavens
there is nothing like your mother.

Notes

1. Carmen Espinosa, "Music Since Coronado," *New Mexico Magazine* 40 (August 1962):21.

2. Translation by Frank V. Mares, May 1989.

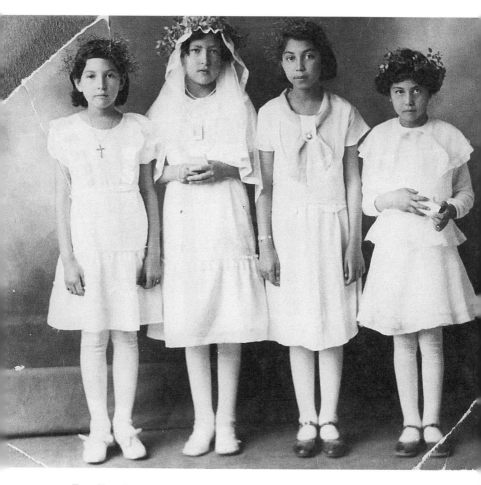

First Holy Communion, St. Francis of Xavier, Albuquerque, 1935. From left, Oralia Leyba, Cristina Griego, Eremita Griego, and Catalina Griego. Photo courtesy of Teodorita García-Ruelas.

CHAPTER 9

ALABADOS, TESTAMENTOS Y ELOGIOS

HYMNS, WILLS, AND EULOGIES

In THIS LAST CHAPTER I EXPLORE THREE INTERRELATED SUBJECTS: hymns, eulogies, and wills. By examining at least one hymn related to death and by considering eulogies and wills, we shall see how and in what ways a loved one's death affected families. Two other hymns, one pertaining to the Passion and death of Christ and the other having to do with man's holy alliance with Christ on earth as well as in heaven, are also discussed briefly.

ALABADOS—HYMNS

Alabados are hymns of praise or passion ballads. They are sometimes referred to as *cuandos*, and they came to New Mexico from Spain via Mexico. While many extant alabados are of Spanish origin, and thus are quite old, others may have originated in Mexico; still others may be of local origin. The use of alabados and other religious practices can be traced to Juan de Oñate's first entrance into New Mexico in 1598. During the nineteenth century, Los Hermanos Penitentes, or the Penitente Brotherhood, employed alabados, but their use has been in decline for quite some time. This trend continues today except in areas where the Penitentes are active. However, as far as the general Hispanic population in small communities is concerned, fewer and fewer people sing them anymore.

"*Alabado sea Dios y todos los santos,*" or "Praise be to God and all of the saints," was an expression my paternal grandmother used from time to time in her prayers on the ranch in Guadalupe. I heard other women and several religious men who were members of the *Cofradía de Nuestro Padre Jesús Nazareno* (Confraternity of Our Father Jesus the Nazarene) use this expression as well. The key word in the phrase is *alabado*, or *alabao* as it is pronounced in New Mexico, and it stems from *alabar*, to praise.

Alabados were sung on different occasions throughout the year in the Río Puerco Valley communities. They were sung during Lent, on Christmas, and on other religious holidays; in honor of the village's patron saint; for special family celebrations; and when someone died.

Adelita Gonzales, a resident of Guadalupe until 1958, was the premier *rezadora* (person known for his or her ability to pray at religious gatherings) in the community, and she was frequently called upon to recite the rosary. She also had a wonderful voice and knew by heart many alabados, some of which were sung at wakes, and it was from her that I obtained the alabados that follow.

In our valley, a resident's death precipitated several activities, ranging from the religious to the social, that ultimately terminated in interment. Although there were no funeral parlors or state and community regulations and procedures by which to abide, the body had to be interred as quickly as possible, especially in the hot summer months. A family's first responsibility was the preparation of the body for the wake, which was followed by a Mass if the priest was available. Following the Mass, the body was interred at the local cemetery.

During the evening of a wake, people arrived, viewed the body, then waited until the rezador(a) began the formal praying session. Typically, the first prayer was the rosary. Sometimes community members offered their condolences to the family prior to the rosary, but as a rule this ritual followed the prayers and singing of hymns. Alabados sung at wakes were sad and mournful. One such alabado that was popular among Río Puerco villagers is *"De las ánimas,"* and it deals with death itself. *"Despedida del sagrado corazón de Jesús"* was sung by the Penitentes on Good Friday after the reenactment of Christ's Crucifixion. *"Alabado sea el Santísimo"* describes the intimate and holy relationship between the worshiper and God, a relationship marked by increasing closeness that culminates in unification.

The alabado was typically written in eight-syllable quatrains with alternate assonated lines (*levantAndO/condenAdO*), although that is not always the case. The number of stanzas for each given alabado in Adelita Gonzales's collection ranges from five to twenty-two. On both counts, this is hardly surprising since we are dealing with the vagaries of the oral tradition.

Unlike dichos and adivinanzas, which are still known to and are practiced by many older people today, alabados have become victims of neglect by old-timers themselves. Elderly people indicate that the neglect is not accidental, for to sing hymns at wakes is to make an already difficult situation all the more painful.

De las ánimas

I
Alma pecadora,
mira adónde vas.
Vuelve atrás los pasos,
no te perderás.
Llora lo pasado.

II
Su conciencia rota,
te trae arrastrando.
Los vicios te tienen
de Dios olvidado.
Llora lo pasado.

III
Llora lo pasado,
mira adónde vas.
Vuelve otra vez los pasos,
no te perderás.
Llora lo pasado.

IV
Si te hubieras muerto,
estando en pecado,
cuán horrible de penas,
te hubieras cercado.
Llora lo pasado.

V
¡Cuántos condenados,
muertos se han hallado!
Sus almas en el infierno,
su cuerpo hurtado.
Llora lo pasado.

VI
Si algún condenado,
al mundo volviera,
que de penitencia,
con tu vida hiciera.
Llora lo pasado.

Concerning the Spirits

I
Sinful soul,
watch where you are going.
Retrace your steps,
and you won't get lost.
Cry for the past.

II
Your troubled conscience,
is pulling you down.
Your sins have made you
forget all about God.
Cry for the past.

III
Cry for the past,
watch where you are going.
Retrace your steps again,
and you won't get lost.
Cry for the past.

IV
If you had died,
while full of sins,
you would have been,
surrounded with sorrow.
Cry for the past.

V
How many condemned,
dead people were found!
Their souls are in hell,
their bodies having fled.
Cry for the past.

VI
If some condemned person,
should return to earth,
and thus use your life,
to make amends and do penance.
Cry for the past.

VII

Bebe con cuidado,
mira adónde vas.
Vuelve atrás tus pasos,
mira adónde vas.
Llora lo pasado.

VIII

Sólo en un segundo,
oh, Rey, te probado.
Saca de este mundo,
ciego, loco, y vano.
Llora lo pasado.

IX

El brazo divino,
se está levantando.
Cuando menos pienses,
serás condenado.
Llora lo pasado.

X

La Iglesia te aclama,
con grande dolor.
Y logremos redama,
hasta la ocasión.
Llora lo pasado.

XI

Si mi Dios te llama,
al dulce reboso.
Confiesa tus culpas,
no seas descuidado.
Llora lo pasado.

XII

Llora lo pasado.
Mira adónde vas,
vuelve atrás los pasos,
no te perderás.

VII

Drink carefully from
whatever table you visit.
Retrace your steps from,
wherever you have been.
Cry for the past.

VIII

Only in a second,
have I proven, oh, King.
Remove from this world
that which is blind, crazy,
and vain.
Cry for the past.

IX

The divine branch,
is elevating itself.
When you least expect it,
you'll be condemned.
Cry for the past.

X

The Church applauds you,
with great grief and pain.
And it sheds tears
for your occasion.
Cry for the past.

XI

If my Lord beckons you,
to His sweet bosom.
Confess your faults,
and don't be careless.
Cry for the past.

XII

Cry for the past.
Watch where you are going,
retrace your steps,
and you won't get lost.

Despedida del sagrado corazón de Jesús

I
Salve corazón abierto,
santa y dulce habitación.
Adiós Jesús de mi vida,
dame vuestra bendición.

II
Salve corazón cargado,
con la cruz de la pasión.
Adiós Jesús de mi vida,
dame vuestra bendición.

III
Salve corazón cruzado,
con nuestro olvido y traición.
Adiós Jesús de mi vida,
dame vuestra bendición.

IV
Adiós amante querido,
dueño de mi corazón.
Adiós Jesús de mi vida,
dame vuestra bendición.

Farewell to Our Sacred Heart of Jesus

I
Hail, oh, open heart,
the sweet and holy bedroom.
Farewell my dear Lord,
please give me your blessing.

II
Hail, oh, heavy heart,
with the Cross of Passion.
Farewell my dear Lord,
please give me your blessing.

III
Oh, save us crossed heart,
from our neglect and deception.
Farewell my dear Lord,
please give me your blessing.

IV
Farewell, oh, dear lover,
possessor of my heart.
Farewell my dear Lord,
please give me your blessing.

Alabado sea el Santísimo

I
Alabado sea el Santísimo,
Sacramento del altar.
En los cielos y en la tierra,
aquí en todo lugar.

II
Alabado sea el Santísimo,
Sacramento del altar.
Y la Virgen concebida,
sin pecado original.

Praise Be to God

I
Praised be the Holy
Sacrament on the altar.
In heaven and on earth,
here and everywhere.

II
Praised be the Holy
Sacrament on the altar.
And to the Virgin conceived,
without any original sin.

III
Angeles y serafines,
ayudarme a bendecir.
A Jesús sacramentado,
que acabo de recibir. *

IV
Sea en el cielo y en la tierra,
alabado sin cesar.
El corazón amoroso,
que hasta mí quiere llegar.

V
Vuestro cuerpo sacrosanto,
benignísimo Señor.
El de fuertes alimentos,
y de débiles vigor.

VI
Vuestro cuerpo sacrosanto,
es mi vida paz y unción.
Es salud y dulce calma,
que mitiga mi dolor.

VII
Vuestro cuerpo sacrosanto,
es suavísima mansión.
Donde el alma opresionada,
goza libre a su amador.

III
Beautiful angels and seraphs,
please help me in blessing.
Our Lord Jesus Christ,
whom I have just received. *

IV
Whether in heaven or on earth,
blessed without ceasing.
Is his loving heart
that wants desperately to reach me.

V
Your most sacrosanct body,
oh exceedingly kind Lord.
You provide nourishment,
to those who are ill and weak.

VI
Your most sacrosanct body,
is my life, peace, and unction.
It is health and sweet calmness,
that mitigates my grief.

VII
Your most sacrosanct body,
is like a very soft mansion.
Where the oppressed soul,
enjoys his lover freely.

*First Holy Communion.

T ESTAMENTOS — W ILLS

Putting money in the bank for retirement as we do today was not something the Río Puercoan did. Most families in the valley were poor, and what little money they had was usually kept by the *agüelita*, or grandmother, who acted as the safety-deposit box for the entire family.

On a higher level, Río Puerco residents believed that only God could safeguard their journey on earth and predict their future. Hence, managing one's destiny was a foolhardy thing to do as far as they were concerned. As they saw it, their fate rested in God's hands.

Similarly, having a will, or *testamento*, was not part of their practice. In older and more traditional families, a legal declaration of a person's desires regarding the disposition of his or her property after death was the exception, not the rule. They saw no practical reason for wills. In the absence of a will there was occasionally something resembling a letter, *como una carta*, and it contained what was willed and to whom. It was the simplest of written documents.

In most cases, when a spouse died, the surviving spouse inherited all of the deceased's possessions. If the wife predeceased the husband, her possessions were to be shared by the couple's offspring, especially the daughters, and it was the husband who distributed the items. When a husband predeceased his wife, the situation changed only if he had indicated specific desires. Such wishes were articulated by the dying on his deathbed in the presence of other family members, but sometimes this was done with only the wife present. It appears that the question of mental competency was not an issue. Regardless of who passed away first, the surviving spouse took firm control of matters.

Most people of the Río Puerco Valley owned only the 160 acres they had homesteaded, their home and possessions therein (furniture, linen, and clothing), livestock and other farm animals, and farm equipment. The will included here underscores the individual's modest possessions, but as has been pointed out, the residents of the Río Puerco Valley were a humble people; this fact alone could explain why they seldom prepared wills.

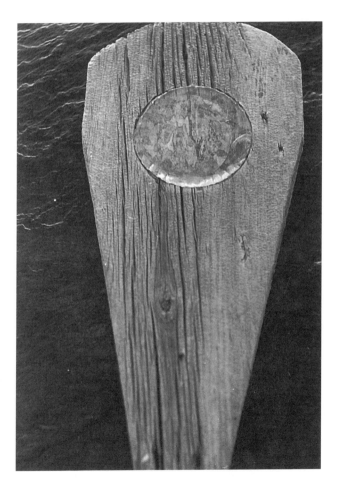

HOMEMADE WOOD "HEADSTONE" WITH GLASS ENCASEMENT FOR NAME OF THE DECEASED. GUADALUPE CEMETERY, 1984. PHOTO BY THE AUTHOR.

TESTAMENTO

EDUMENIO LOVATO

En el nombre de Dios. Amén.
Yo Felipe Lobato de la plaza de San Luis,
en el arriba dicho condado y territorio
[Sandoval y Nuevo Méjico].

Estando bueno y sano de mi mente y memoria. Gracias a Dios
Todo Poderoso. Hago este mi último Testamento y Voluntad. Le
doy, y le dejo a mi querida esposa Nasarita Ruiz de Lobato toda
la propiedad, raíz, y personal que ahora poseo o pueda poseer y
consiste de dos casas o quizas y terreno. Una llegua y tres
caballos con este fierro FL *todo ajuera de casa. Y toda otra*
propieda de la cual ahora tengo o en lo futuro pueda tener.

Yo nombro a mi dicha esposa ejecutora sola, y con todo derecho de
administrar en mi dicho estado en este mi último testamento. En
testimonio de lo cual pongo en puño y sello, y publico, y declaro
este de ser mi última voluntad y testamento en precencia de los
testigos abajo firmados. Hoy este día 31 de Diciembre A.D. *1910.*

Felipe Lobato

Firmado, sellado, declarado y publicado por el dicho Felipe
Lobato, como su último, Testamento y voluntad en precencia de
nosotros y a su suplica y en su precencia y precencia de
nosotros, hemos firmado como testigos.

Delbo Martínez
Casimiro Mestas

Hoy este día 31 de Diciembre A.D. *1910*
personalmente comparecio Felipe Lobato a mi bien y personal-
mente conocido a hacer la misma persona esta firmada en la
antecedente testamento y voluntad y declara que ha firmado de su
entero conocimiento y voluntad, y para los fines en el contenido.
11:50 A.M.

C. W. Holiman
Notario Público

WILL

EDUMENIO LOVATO

In the name of God. Amen.
I Felipe Lobato from the village of San Luis,
on the abovementioned county and territory
[Sandoval and New Mexico].

Being sound and healthy both in mind and spirit, thanks be to God almighty, I draw up this last will of my own volition. I give to my dear wife Nasarita Ruiz de Lobato all of the property, rudimentary and personal, that I now possess or may possess which consists of two houses, more or less, and land; a mare and three horses with this brand, FL, all apart from the house. And all of the other property that I now have or that I may have in the future.

I name my wife the sole executrix, with every right to administer due to my present health conditions according to this my last will. I swear by what I put forth by virtue of my own hand and seal, and which I make public, and I declare this to be my last effort and will in the presence of the witnesses whose signatures appear below. Today the 31st of December A.D. 1910.

Felipe Lobato

Signed, sealed, made manifest and public by the aforementioned Felipe Lobato, as his last will of his own accord in our presence and at his behest and in his presence as well as ours, we here signed as witnesses.

Delbo Martínez
Casimiro Mestas

On this day, the 31st of December A.D., 1910, Felipe Lobato personally came before me and [he is] personally known to be the same person who has affixed his signature in the foregoing will of his own volition and affirms that he has signed in full recognition of and of his own free will, the stipulations contained herein. 11:50 A.M.

C. W. Holiman
Notary Public

MARIANITO APODACA, GUADALUPE, N.M., C. 1904. PHOTO COURTESY OF THE AUTHOR.

ELOGIOS — EULOGIES

Formal praise of the deceased came in the form of *elogios*, or eulogies, at the graveside, and they were of a religious as well as secular nature. If a burial coincided with the priest's monthly visit to the village, he delivered a eulogy in the church; other times he did so at the graveside. It was not uncommon for a family member, friend, or individual from the community to recite a eulogy composed for the occasion.

The only eulogy in my possession is that which follows. It was written by a personal friend of the deceased and not by a village scribe. The author, whose name was not provided, wrote this without any input from the family. In it he acknowledges that the deceased, Edumenio Lovato's mother, was a good wife and mother and thus fulfilled her sacramental responsibilities.

CRECENCIO SALAS, LAST GUADALUPE RESIDENT TO BE BURIED IN THE VILLAGE BEFORE ITS DEMISE IN 1958. PHOTO BY THE AUTHOR, 1984.

ELOGIO

EDUMENIO LOVATO

Febrero 1937

Mi muy querido y desdichado amigo. Señores y Señoras.

Nuestras lágrimas son más elocuentes que todo lo que yo pudiera decir, pero quiero rendir un homenaje a la digna esposa que vamos a confiar a la tumba, y a intentar dulcificar por la expresión de nuestro sentimiento el inconsolable dolor de este padre y estos huérfanos.

He aquí, sin duda, la primera aflicción que nuestra desdichada amiga ha causado a los suyos. ¡Qué cruel! Que falta hacía que los que fueron dignos de afección y amor lleven en sus corazones los golpes más terribles en la hora de la eterna separación. Es muy fácil ver todo lo que la muerte nos revela y comprender cuán irreparable es semejante pérdida.

Sí, mi querido amigo. Nuestro pensamiento pone al unísono del tuyo y de tus recuerdos, y sabemos las tierras y dolorosas imágenes que surgen de tu corazón y ocupan tu memoria. Tú ves de nuevo la graciosa joven que en otro tiempo puso su mano en la tuya. Que prometió ser tu compañera y darte dicha. Sabes demasiado bien que ha cumplido su palabra hasta el fin. Y es lo que hace redoblar los sollozos.

Después la ves inclinada sobre la cuna de tus hijos, siempre vigilante y consagrada; dichosa de multiplicar para ellos los cuidados y los sacrificios y dedicarse a ellos un poco más cada día. Hoy lloran contigo porque su madre no existe y no quieren ser consolados.

La dulce imagen de la que ya no existe, ocupa siempre tu pensamiento. De allá únicamente obtendrás algún consuelo y conseguirás fuerzas para vivir. Cuando el invencible abatimiento

EULOGY

EDUMENIO LOVATO

February 1937

My Very Dear and Unfortunate Friend. Ladies and Gentlemen.

Our tears are much more eloquent than anything I could ever say, but I offer a eulogy to the worthy wife whom we entrust to the grave, and I also attempt to sweeten, via the expression of our grief, the inconsolable sorrow of this father and these children.

Here you have, without doubt, the first affliction that our friend has brought to her loved ones. How cruel! There was no need for those who were so worthy of love and affection to carry in their hearts the most terrible blows in the hour of eternal separation. It is very easy to see everything death reveals to us and to understand how irreparable such a loss is.

Yes, my dear friend. Our thoughts are united with your memories, and we know the territory and the painful images that surge from your heart and occupy your mind. You see once again the gracious young lady who in times past put her hand in yours, who promised to be your companion and to give you happiness. You know very well that she complied with her word to the end. And that is what makes us repeat our sighs.

Then you see her bent over your children's cradle, always watchful and devoted, happily increasing her caring, making sacrifices for them, and dedicating herself to them more and more each day. Today they weep with you because their mother no longer exists, and they refuse to be consoled.

The sweet image of the one who no longer exists is always in your mind. From her alone you shall obtain some consolation and derive strength to live. When the invincible depression of (t)he first few days has dissipated a little, you shall think that you have

de los primeros días está un poco disipado, pensarás que has partido la primera, y que, por lo menos, no tendrá como tú, las tristezas de la viudez.

Tu terrible desdicha encontrará un consuelo en el pensamiento de que ella no habrá conocido los días solitarios que tú vivirás. Y después de haberlo compartido con ella serás dichoso de ella guardar para ti tan solo pena.

Después, con el recuerdo de sus virtudes y de su incansable sacrificio te deja a la guarda de estos tus hijos en los que revive lo mejor de ella, su viviente imagen y su amor. Su caricia te recordarán las suyas. Su afección será tu más seguro reconfortante y el bálsamo más eficaz para cicatrizar la herida que tienes en el fondo de tu corazón.

THE PENITENTES ON THEIR WAY TO CALVARY ON GOOD FRIDAY, SAN LUIS, N.M. DATE UNKNOWN. PHOTO COURTESY OF SALOMÓN LOVATO.

overcome the initial shock and [you will realize that] she, unlike you, will not have the sadness of widowhood.

Your terrible misfortune shall encounter consolation in thinking that she will not know the lonely days you shall live. And after you have shared it with her, you shall be well advised to keep such grief to yourself.

Afterwards, with the memory of her virtue and her untiring sacrifice, she leaves you with the care of your children in whom the best part of her comes alive: her vibrant image and love. Her affection will remind you of yours. Her affection shall be your most reassuring comfort and the most efficacious balsam to heal the wound in the bottom of your heart.

This chapter brings to a close an exploration of folklore from the Río Puerco Valley. With the demise of Cabezón, Guadalupe, Casa Salazar, and San Luis, people abandoned their homes and many of their social and religious customs. What they carried with them to their new place of residence in the Río Grande Valley was minuscule in comparison to what they possessed as their raison d'être in the Río Puerco Valley. What they left for us and for future generations to enjoy are irreplaceable and long-lasting treasures of New Mexican folklore. For this we are grateful.

Los Comanches de Guadalupe, N.M., 1930—Children who put on plays at Christmastime. Photo courtesy of Inesita Márez-Tafoya.

Apéndice

Appendix

The Spanish dialect of the Río Puerco Valley reflects archaisms, whose linguistic roots lie in Spain, as in *mesmo* for *mismo* (same), *vide* for *vi* (saw), and *truje* for *traje* (brought); regionalisms, the product of local pronunciation or invention, as in *persicutando* for *persiguiendo* (pursuing); and Anglicisms, such as *troca* for truck and *juisque* for whiskey, which infiltrated the valley and were adopted as part of the people's lexicon. Some terms, such as *penitensaron* (sent to prison), appear to be indigenous to the valley as they are not found outside the Río Puerco Valley.

This appendix juxtaposes a regional term with a modern or standard version, but one must bear in mind that what is deemed nonstandard Spanish by an outsider was indeed standard lexicon for the local speaker. Moreover, the words listed here show one of two things or both: the manner in which valley denizens pronounced certain words and the way in which these words were written in documents such as entriegas, corridos, and chiquiaos. Other orthographic or pronunciation features that were prevalent in the Río Puerco Valley may have their sources in Spain or Mexico, or they may be products of the population's own linguistic invention. Words such as *abuelo, bueno, mucho, fuerte, volver,* and *nada* were pronounced in the Río Puerco Valley as a*güelo, güeno, muncho, juerte, golver,* and *naa,* and this is how most are pronounced in Andalucía, Spain. The double *ll* of *ella* or *gallina* is pronounced in New Mexico as a *y* sound, hence the pronunciation *eya* and *gayina.* Such is the case in several regions of Spain. In some parts of Northern New Mexico and southern Colorado, the *ll* is lost entirely, and so the word *allí* is pronounced *ahi* or *ai.* Archaisms, such as *anque* for *aunque, cuasi* for *casi,* and *dijieron* for *dijeron,* are heard from time to time in Spain and are still with us in New Mexico. This is probably due to the isolated state New Mexico found itself in after the Treaty of Guadalupe Hidalgo of 1848 when the United States took possession of the region. Finally, a word about the letters *b* and *v.* It is not unusual among old-timers in New Mexico to hear the initial *v* or intervocalic *v* both pronounced and spelled as a *b.* Some old folks may also pronounce the *v* as a *v.*

REGIONAL	STANDARD	REGIONAL	STANDARD
A		agradesco	agradezco
abía(s)	había(s)	agüelito(a)	abuelito(a)
acarriaba	acarreaba	agüelo(a)	abuelo(a)
a en papá	a mi papá	aguilez	agilidad
aferrao	aferrado	ahi	allí
agan	hagan	ai	allí

REGIONAL	STANDARD	REGIONAL	STANDARD
airiento	airoso	comparecio	compareció
ajuera	afuera	conforme	según
ajuero	agujero	conocemiento	conocimiento
alasana	alazana	conocites	conociste
almuada	almohada	conosimiento	conocimiento
amarrao	amarrado	corrigidor	corregidor
anque	aunque	cortao	cortado
apreviniendo	preparando	criábanos	criábamos
arquerir	adquerir	cuasi	casi
arrogansa	arrogancia	cute	abrigo
asegún	según		
asen	hacen	**D**	
aser	hacer	decición	decisión
asero	acero	dejate	déjate
atenerse	fiarse	dél	de él
atrás	detrás	d'ellos	de ellos
atuen	actúen	d'en	de en
a'ullar	a aullar	derigir	dirigir
ay	he	desfender	defender
		desfendía	defendía
B		despidemos	despedimos
balansa	balanza	d'esta	de esta
benías	venías	destendieron	extendieron
bersitos	versitos	destendió	extendió
beses	veces	d'estos	de estos
bibo	vivo	deven	deben
bolar	volar	dever	deber
boluntad(es)	voluntad(es)	dia	día
bonche	montón	dicía(n)	decía(n)
		dijía(n)	decía(n)
C		dijiendo	diciendo
caiban	caían	dijieron	dijeron
caidrá	caerá	dijunta(o)	difunta(o)
chimineya	chiminea	diónde	donde
chosa	choza	diós	Dios
coletando	colectando	disfigurado	desfigurado
companía(s)	compañía(s)	disierto	desierto

REGIONAL	STANDARD	REGIONAL	STANDARD
dispénsemen	dispénsenme	**G**	
dites	diste	galopiando	galopeando
duélancen	duélansen	garrotiao	garroteado
		Genobeba	Genoveva
E		goteya	gotea
echales	echarles	gotiaba	goteaba
echiceros	hechiceros	gotiando	goteando
echisito	exquisito	güen	buen
elejir	elegir	güena	buena
elétrica	eléctrica	güeno(s)	bueno(s)
embolancita	ambulancita		
embolao	embolado	**H**	
embolaron	embor-	ha	he
	racharon	haiga(n)	haya(n)
en papá	mi papá	herrao(s)	herrado(s)
engremiento	engreimiento	hijados	ahijados
entegridad	integridad	hora	ahora
entregao	entregado		
envestigar	investigar	**I**	
éranos	éramos	iglecia	iglesia
escojido	escogido	illendo	yendo
escusao	excusado	inmienda	enmienda
espirar	expirar	inotomía	crueldad
esplicar	explicar	isque	dizque
esque	dizque		
estábanos	estábamos	**J**	
est'agua	esta agua	jalló	halló
estilla	astilla	jedentina	hedentina
estraña(s)	extraña(s)	jiede	hiede
estreyas	estrellas	jue	fue
		juella	huella
F		juera	fuera
faborable	favorable	jueron	fueron
fierro	hierro	juerte	fuerte
fletiaba	fletaba	jui	fui
fletiábanos	fletábamos	jurao	jurado
fuistes	fuiste		
		K	

REGIONAL	STANDARD	REGIONAL	STANDARD
L		**O**	
lao	lado	onde	donde
lasos	lazos	ónde	dónde
lave	el ave	ondequiera	dondequiera
l'hacha	el hacha	ora	(a)hora
lión	león	ordenes	órdenes
liones	leones	óygame	óigame
lla	ya		
llege	llegue		
llegua	yegua	**P**	
llevábanos	llevábamos	pa	para
llo	yo	paderes	paredes
loo	luego	pagábanos	pagábamos
		pais	país
M		pal	para el
maiz	maíz	pallá	para allá
matao	matado	panza	estómago
medianita	chiquita	papel	periódico
megor	mejor	pardo	gris
Méjico	México	partisipando	participando
méndigo	mendigo	patrás	para atrás
mesma	misma	peliaba	peleaba
mesmo	mismo	peliando	peleando
m'hijito	mi hijito	peliar	pelear
Miliano	Emiliano	penitensaron	encarcelaron
muchito(a)	muchachito(a)	persicutando	persiguiendo
muebas	muevas	pesao	pesado
muncho(a)	mucho(a)	pidir	pedir
		pilalo	apilarlo
N		plan	centro
nación	nacionalidad	plebe	niños
nadien	nadie	ponarán	pondrán
naide	nadie	precencia	presencia
nececidá	necesidad	probe(s)	pobre(s)
necitábanos	necesitábamos	propriedá	propiedad
noo	nuevo	proveza	pobreza
nuevecientos	novecientos	pueta	poeta
ñudo	nudo	pus	pues

MEANDERING RÍO PUERCO NEAR GUADALUPE, N.M. PHOTO BY THE AUTHOR, 1996.

APIÉNDICE / APPENDIX

183

REGIONAL	STANDARD	REGIONAL	STANDARD
		telégrafas	telégrafos
Q		teníanos	teníamos
quadrillas	cuadrillas	tirastes	tiraste
quizas	quizás	tiñiste	teñiste
		toparon	encontraron
R		tostón	cincuenta
recibites	recibiste		centavos
recivites	recibiste	traiba(n)	traía(n)
rededor	alrededor	tresquilaban	trasquilaban
redució	redujo	troca	camión;
relampaguiando	relampagueando		camioneta
reló	reloj	truje	traje
respetosamente	respetuosamente	trujo	trajo
resulución	resolusión	tu	tú
riyendo	riendo	tullas	tuyas
rodeao	rodeado		
		U	
S		un'hacha	una hacha
salites	saliste	usté	usted
seguido	frecuentemente		
Selima	Seligman	**V**	
sella(n)	sea(n)	valla	vaya
sembrábanos	sembrábamos	veses	veces
senifican	significan	vía	veía
sentido	mente	vide	vi
serbidores	servidores	vido	vio
siguemos	seguimos	viéranos	viéramos
siguí	seguí	vinía	venía
siguir	seguir	voltiar	voltear
siguiremos	seguiremos	voltió	volteó
sintería	sentiría	voluntá	voluntad
so	solo		
sotella	azotea	**W**	
sumición	sumisión	Winislow	Winslow
T		**X**	
tamién	también	**Y**	
tardábanos	tardábamos	**Z**	

Frank V. Mares and his mother, Bruna Valencia
Mares, Albuquerque, 1977. Photo courtesy of
Frank V. Mares.

Edumenio Lovato, Los
Griegos (Albuquerque),
N.M., 1990. Photo by
the author.

CONTRIBUIDORES

CONTRIBUTORS

LUCINDA ATENCIO*

Born: July 14, 1894
Cañón, New Mexico
Sandoval County
Died: November 24, 1978
Albuquerque, New Mexico
Bernalillo County

ADRIÁN CHÁVEZ

Born: December 15, 1913
Albuquerque (Armijo),
New Mexico
Bernalillo County
Residence: Albuquerque,
New Mexico
Bernalillo County

* Passed away in an Albuquerque hospital but was a resident of
Bernalillo for many years prior to her death.

VICENTITA CHÁVEZ

Born: May 5, 1913
Guadalupe, New Mexico
Sandoval County
Residence: Albuquerque,
New Mexico
Bernalillo County

NASARIO P. GARCÍA

Born: September 10, 1912
Guadalupe (Rincón del
Cochino), New Mexico
Sandoval County
Residence: Albuquerque
(Los Ranchos de
Albuquerque), New Mexico
Bernalillo County

TEODORO GARCÍA

Born: November 3, 1872
Algodones, New Mexico
Sandoval County
Died: September 12, 1972
Albuquerque (Martínez Town),
New Mexico
Bernalillo County

ADELITA GONZALES

Born: June 11, 1909
Guadalupe, New Mexico
Sandoval County
Died: February 20, 1990
Albuquerque, New Mexico
Bernalillo County

AGAPITA LÓPEZ-GARCÍA

Born: September 18, 1919
San Miguel, New Mexico
Sandoval County
Died: May 25, 1972
Albuquerque, New Mexico
Bernalillo County

EDUMENIO LOVATO

Born: February 12, 1913
San Luis, New Mexico
Sandoval County
Died: November 4, 1995
Albuquerque, New Mexico
Bernalillo County

SALOMÓN LOVATO

Born: April 4, 1915
San Luis, New Mexico
Sandoval County
Residence: Albuquerque,
New Mexico
Bernalillo County

BENJAMÍN ("BENNY") LUCERO

Born: June 29, 1924
Cabezón, New Mexico
Sandoval County
Residence: Albuquerque,
New Mexico
Bernalillo County

DAMIANO ROMERO

Born: June 4, 1916
Casa Salazar, New Mexico
Sandoval County
Died: February 22, 1984
Albuquerque, New Mexico

SIFREDO ROMERO

Born: June 4, 1917
Casa Salazar
Sandoval County
Residence: Algodones,
New Mexico
Sandoval County

EDUARDO VALDEZ

Born: October, 26, 1908
Guadalupe, New Mexico
Sandoval County
Died: May 11, 1987
Bernalillo, New Mexico
Sandoval County

ANTOÑITA VALDEZ DE LEYBA

Born: January 8, 1899
El Llanito, New Mexico
Sandoval County
Died: June 9, 1989
Bernalillo, New Mexico
Sandoval County

BRUNA VALENCIA MARES

Born: November 8, 1892
Casa Salazar, New Mexico
Sandoval County
Died: August 11, 1978
Albuquerque, New Mexico
Bernalillo County

SIFREDO ROMERO, RANCHER
AND PROPERTY OWNER IN
GUADALUPE, N.M. PHOTO
TAKEN IN ALGODONES, N.M., IN
1993 BY THE AUTHOR.